D1648519

ROBERT DINWIDDIE

Williamsburg in America Series

IX

*The ninth in a series of popular histories
focusing on the roles of Williamsburg and Virginia
in the eighteenth century*

ROBERT DINWIDDIE

Servant of the Crown

by

John Richard Alden

The Colonial Williamsburg Foundation
Williamsburg, Virginia

Distributed by
The University Press of Virginia
Charlottesville, Virginia

© 1973 by
The Colonial Williamsburg Foundation
All rights reserved

12- 13-74

Library of Congress Catalog Card Number: 72–86731
Colonial Williamsburg ISBN: 0–87935–002–4
University Press of Virginia ISBN: 0–8139–0440–4

Printed in the United States of America

Contents

List of Illustrations

Preface

This biographical study covers the career of colonial Virginia's Governor Robert Dinwiddie, native of Glasgow, erstwhile and respected merchant, and veteran servant of the British crown. He was a hospitable man, and he was connected by marriage with influential Virginia families, the Nelsons, the Corbins, and the Tuckers. Even so, his tenure in the "Palace" at Williamsburg was not easy and comfortable. As governor he sent young George Washington to challenge the French advancing in the Ohio valley, and he played an important role in precipitating the great struggle for empire in North America known on this side of the Atlantic as the French and Indian War. He was responsible in considerable degree for the expedition that General Edward Braddock led to tragic defeat in the western wilderness. He wept over the sad news of that disaster, and he sorrowfully read many reports of French and Indian raids on the frontiers of the Old Dominion. He left Williamsburg before the tide of war turned, before Canada fell to the arms of Generals James Wolfe and Jeffery Amherst.

But the period during which Dinwiddie held office at Williamsburg was remarkable for more than warfare. We are accustomed to believe that the treaty of Paris of the year 1763 marked not only the end of the French empire in North America but the beginning of the era of the American Revolution. Nevertheless quarrels that arose in Virginia in Dinwiddie's time portended Anglo-American strife soon to come, conflicts in which Virginians protested bitterly against the taking of their money without their consent by British officials. Historians have frequently remarked that Dinwiddie's attempt to collect the notorious pistole fee on land patents, without the

ix

approval of the House of Burgesses, was considered tyrannical by many Virginians. Much more serious constitutionally was his expenditure of Virginia tax money for imperial purposes, acting—on two occasions—on orders of the British ministry and without the consent of the burgesses. Despite protests from Dinwiddie, Britain took money from the pockets of the Virginians without concern for their established rights, foreshadowing the acts that ultimately goaded the Thirteen Colonies into revolt against the mother country.

Let it not be thought that Dinwiddie, befriending the young Washington, gave his heart to Virginia. His allegiance was always to Britain, and his vexatious experiences in America convinced him that the colonists must be brought to heel, that Parliament ought to tax them for revenue. He was an old-school imperialist. Indeed, after leaving Virginia, he urged upon the earl of Bute, the British prime minister, the necessity and wisdom of imposing stamp duties on the Americans by act of Parliament. He had some little share in the shaping of British measures that provoked the rebellion of the colonists and led to the creation of the American republic. Spending the last years of his life in Britain, he did not live long enough to witness the birth of the American nation.

I am grateful for the assistance given me by the Duke University Research Council; for gracious courtesies extended to me by the British Public Record Office, the British Museum, the Institute of Historical Research of London, the library of the University of Glasgow, the Virginia Historical Society, the William L. Clements Library, the Library of Congress, and the Henry E. Huntington Library and Art Gallery; and for helpful services rendered by Mr. Noël Dinwiddie, Mrs. Elizabeth D. Holladay, the Reverend Mr. Robert H. Hyslop, Mrs. Vivian Jackson, Mr. J. D. Kilgore, Mr. Robert C. Law, Mr. Howard H. Peckham, and Mr. Terry Tucker. I gladly testify that essential help was generously given me by Dr. Edward M. Riley, Mr. Thomas K. Ford, Mr. Vernon Wooten, and other members of the staff of Colonial Williamsburg.

John R. Alden

Chapter 1
An Enterprising Scot

According to a rumor that circulated in Williamsburg before the end of May 1751, His Majesty George II had selected Robert Dinwiddie to be chief executive of the Old Dominion. Virginians received the report with pleasure, not so much because they already knew Dinwiddie as an energetic colonial official with influential friends in London, but rather because the colony had been struggling along without a governor for two years.

Dinwiddie was in England at the time. Not until July did a letter "confirming our hopes of Mr. Dinwiddie's coming," as John Blair wrote in his diary, reach John Robinson, speaker of the Virginia House of Burgesses. Toward the end of that month the new governor's arrival at Yorktown was "daily expected," but it was November 20 before Blair could record "Govr on Shoar." Dinwiddie's wife and two daughters came with him.

The following day the governor rode over from Yorktown to make his formal appearance in the capital city. Five members of the Council of Virginia went out to meet him and escort him into the town. At the city limits the mayor and aldermen awaited to take him and the councilors to dinner at Wetherburn's Tavern. Afterwards the welcoming party accompanied him to a house that had been rented for him where he produced his commission, made a speech, and took his oath of office.

Returning to Yorktown, he brought his wife and daughters to Williamsburg the next day. On November 23 Mr. and Mrs. Blair were guests of the Dinwiddies at dinner. Blair wrote in his diary that "many ladies and gentn visited them in the afternoon, and were highly pleasd with them." So as pleasantly as might be, Robert Dinwiddie assumed his duties as acting governor, captain general, and vice admiral of Virginia.

The first citizen of Williamsburg and Virginia for more than six years thereafter, Dinwiddie did not remain popular— few royal governors departed from America amidst acclaim such as they received on taking office. An able and worthy man, he made many and potent enemies in the Old Dominion. He fought loyally for the Anglican church and for the crown. He forthrightly challenged the French when they sought to establish themselves on the headwaters of the Ohio River and to bar English westward expansion; and he precipitated the mighty conflict of the Seven Years' War. Devoted and endlessly toiling, but aging and ailing, he did all he could to defend Virginia and to encompass the defeat of the French.

His sacrifices for Virginia and for Britain were neither as highly appreciated in the mother country as they might have been nor valued by all citizens of the colony. George Washington, for one, began his rise to fame under the patronage of Dinwiddie but turned against him. Setting sail for Britain before the collapse of the French, the governor left behind friends who mourned his departure and enemies glad to see him go.

Robert Dinwiddie was one of those Scots who contributed so much to Britain after the union of England and Scotland in 1707 and who were so detested by jealous Englishmen through the rest of the eighteenth century. Scotsmen swarming into London to seek their fortune gave offense by their brogue, their sycophancy, their clannishness; and many generations of Englishmen have enjoyed the witty thrusts at the Scots delivered by Dr. Samuel Johnson and John Wilkes. But it ought not be forgotten that able and industrious Scots aroused the irritation of idle, frivolous, privileged, and provincial-minded English noblemen by display of merit as well as by offering sharp competition for preferment in government and commerce. Of such was Dinwiddie, who was not of noble birth, even of the Scottish variety. In later life he laid claim to a family crest with the motto, *Ubi libertas, ibi patria*— "Where there is liberty, there is my country." Dr. Johnson would have insisted that *libertas* ought to have been *pecunia* —"money."

The governor-to-be was one of at least nine children of Robert Dinwiddie, merchant, of Glasgow. His mother was Elizabeth Cumming, daughter of another merchant, albeit Matthew Cumming of Carderock was also at one time a bailie —a judge—of Glasgow. It may well be, as genealogists suggest, that both parents were descended from important land-owning families, and that the governor was technically entitled to his crest. The Dinwiddies lived at Dumfries before they settled in Glasgow, but it is apparent that the future governor was not born a country gentleman.

That does not mean the young man was deprived of education or opportunity. At the time of his birth, on October 3, 1692, his father owned a seat called Germiston outside Glasgow. The older Dinwiddie was wealthy enough early in the eighteenth century to invest £500 in the Darien enterprise, that ill-fated attempt by speculative Scots to establish a colony in Panama. He was also able to send Robert and his younger brother, Lawrence, to the University of Glasgow.

"Robertus Dinwiddie" entered that institution as a student in 1707. He had John Law as his tutor—not the famous John Law who afterward severely damaged the finances of France by reckless management but a professor of moral philosophy who presumably did not encourage the boys under his direction to gamble in stocks or in any other way. Robert graduated from the university, probably in 1710 or 1711; his *alma mater* later gave him two honorary degrees. It cannot be said that he excelled remarkably in scholarship, though he was doubtless a faithful student.

The university, small as it then was, offered its students opportunity to gain classical and even liberal learning; but it is to be suspected that Dinwiddie learned more about ethics from John Law than he did about metaphysics, and that in maturity he devoted his energies almost exclusively to private and public business rather than cultural pursuits. His extensive official correspondence contains hardly a hint of classical or liberal learning.

After Dinwiddie had left the university, one of its professors, John Anderson, a wit, put forth the proposition "That an university is rather a hurt than an advantage to a trading town for it has been universally observed of the merchants of

Glasgow that the most ignorant of them have been the most successful." Dinwiddie was indeed successful. He was not ignorant in later life, but his writings are those of a man seeking to save time, of an energetic man of affairs; he was fond of abbreviations, not too observant of syntax. As governor of Virginia he came forth as a champion of education; but he was not acclaimed as a man of learning.

The Dinwiddie family encountered financial reverses after, if not before, Robert left the university. His father suffered losses in property before his death, in 1712. His eldest brother, Matthew, inherited Germiston but was unable to keep it and in 1738 became an inmate of the Merchants' House, a home maintained by businessmen for the poor of Glasgow.

Most of Robert's other siblings failed to achieve fortune or fame. At least two of his sisters married Scottish clergymen. Another, an emigrant to Pennsylvania, became the wife of a certain Andrew Stuart and the mother of the distinguished Dr. John Stuart, Anglican missionary to the Mohawk Indians, prominent Loyalist, and a principal figure in early Ontario. An older brother, John, settled on the Rappahannock River in Virginia, married into the famous Mason family, and became a progenitor of many prominent Americans. Appointed sheriff of King and Queen County, he achieved the rank of "gentleman" in Virginia before his death.

Lawrence Dinwiddie, a younger brother, born in 1697, achieved success second only to that of Robert. He matriculated at the University of Glasgow in 1709, became a merchant in his native place, fathered twenty-one children, and eventually prospered with respect to cash as well as progeny. He purchased Germiston house in 1748. Becoming one of the principal citizens of Glasgow, he thrice served as its lord provost—its mayor.

It has been surmised, no doubt correctly, that Robert Dinwiddie went into trade immediately after finishing his studies at the University of Glasgow, less certainly that he began his mercantile career in the counting house of his father. Actually, nothing is positively known about him during the eight years that followed his graduation from the university. However, after the close of the long War of the Spanish Succession in 1713 Glasgow merchants began to engage extensively in maritime commerce and flourished. Two of those active in overseas trade were Robert's brothers Lawrence and Matthew.

The first vessel from Glasgow to engage in American business sailed from that port, according to one account, in 1718. Possibly Robert Dinwiddie had somewhat to do with that voyage. In any event, James Cheape, a Scottish businessman, writing from London in August of that year to his friend Cadwallader Colden in Philadelphia, reported that he had recently visited Glasgow acquaintances, that he was about to sail on a voyage to Holland, Africa, and Virginia in their service, and that "Mr. Robert Dinwiedies & I are just drinking your lady's health & yours & he gives his humble service to both." Was Dinwiddie to accompany Cheape? No answer to that question can be given. It is certain that he was a resident soon afterward of Bermuda.

The future governor was unquestionably well established in Bermuda before he reached the age of 30. The small islets of that colony, then containing not many more than eight thousand people, almost half of whom were Negro slaves, offered a splendid climate rather than enticing economic opportunity. Dinwiddie, however, was both enterprising and canny. He may also have been, like the stereotyped Scot, thrifty in youth, although he was liberal enough with money in his later years.

A man could make money by building vessels in the "Summer Islands," as Bermuda was sometimes called, and carrying goods, especially salt, to the West Indies and the mainland of North America; "Capn. Robert Dinwiddie Esqr." engaged in such ventures. Edmund Randolph later asserted that Dinwiddie was "the master of a little vessel trading in the rivers" of Virginia. Clearly Dinwiddie made at least one voyage to Newfoundland, where salt and codfish could be profitably combined for consumption elsewhere. He also bought and sold goods at a counting house he acquired on the seaside in St. George's parish. In 1725 Bermudians owed him more than £5,000. Apparently he managed to collect all those debts, including suitable interest, without acquiring a reputation as a Scottish Shylock. Eventually he became the richest man in St. George's parish, "the most substantial man of business in Bermuda."

Rising to wealth, Dinwiddie acquired good repute and influential friends, not only in Bermuda but in London. And he made use of his friends to secure public offices. How he became *persona grata* to the British navy remains unknown, but he somehow obtained an appointment on September 1, 1721, as agent in Bermuda for the "Receiver General and Solicitor and Comptroller of the rights and perquisites of Admiralty." Just what "rights and perquisites" the Admiralty possessed in Bermuda also remains a mystery.

The commission aroused the resentment of the governor of Bermuda, Colonel John Bruce Hope, a fellow Scot, an officer who had served under the duke of Marlborough and Charles XII of Sweden. Governor Hope as vice admiral, received perquisites arising from the seizure of ships and cargoes taken from merchants who violated British laws concerning maritime trade, notably smugglers. He had no intention of abandoning his rights to Dinwiddie and protested to the home government that "There never was any such commission here before" and that other governors whom he had consulted had never heard of such an appointment.

Some weeks later, Hope learned that a mass of ambergris, that expulsion from the stomach of the whale which was so valuable in the making of perfume in the eighteenth century, had come ashore, and that it had fallen into the possession of the new agent of the Admiralty. He took Dinwiddie for a stroll. Was the report true? If so, Dinwiddie had no right to keep the small treasure. Dinwiddie replied that he did not have the ambergris; were it in his hands, he would keep it. But the governor was ultimately victorious. The appointment of Dinwiddie was obviously an act of usurpation by the Admiralty, and it was set aside in London.

In the heat of his controversy with Dinwiddie, Governor Hope made an uncomplimentary remark about his antagonist. He had, Hope reported, some reason to suspect Dinwiddie of concealing the ambergris because of "his practices that way, before he was dignified by this commission; for Govr. Bennet during his government took a parcel from him which he had clandestinely purchased." But, whatever those peccadilloes were—if indeed they existed—Hope changed his mind about Dinwiddie. By 1725 Dinwiddie had become "an intimate friend" of the governor. Hope quarreled with the collector of customs in Bermuda and secured his discharge; he was, said Hope, in the habit of remaining drunk for five or six weeks at a stretch. Dinwiddie, probably with the consent of the governor, perhaps even at his recommendation, was appointed to the office by Horatio Walpole, brother of the British prime minister, Sir Robert Walpole. Horatio Walpole had been given—and retained until his death in 1757—the right to choose all customs officers serving in North America and the West Indies. If Dinwiddie was not then a protege of Horatio Walpole, he became one at a later time.

Dinwiddie certainly also remained in the good graces of John Bruce Hope, for the governor urged in 1726 that Dinwiddie be made a member of the Council of Bermuda. The Council, in accordance with British custom in the royal colonies, was at once a confidential body advising the governor, the upper house of the Bermuda assembly, and the island colony's high court. The recommendation was not heeded, but Hope repeated it in 1730, after he had resigned as governor and returned to England, and the government then complied with his wishes. Dinwiddie's entrance into the Council signified that he had become politically and socially select as well as prosperous. He remained on the Council until his departure from Bermuda a decade later.

The flourishing businessman and rising official of the crown also married well in Bermuda. Precisely when he took Rebecca Auchinleck to wife cannot be ascertained, but the wedding was solemnized some time before 1738. Dinwiddie was apparently more than forty years of age when he finally assumed the responsibilities of a family. His wife was doubtless much younger than he. She bore him two daughters, Elizabeth in 1738 and Rebecca about four years later.

The union of Robert Dinwiddie and Rebecca Auchinleck was a happy one; it also fostered his career as a public servant. Mrs. Dinwiddie was the only child of the Reverend Andrew Auchinleck, the principal Anglican clergyman in Bermuda— for some years in fact the only representative of the English established church in the colony. A worthy and amiable man of God, much respected and loved in the islands, Auchinleck became a member of the Council in 1722 and served three times as chief executive of the colony in the absence of a governor. The mother of Mrs. Dinwiddie, also named Rebecca, was a daughter of a merchant captain, John Tucker, member of a numerous and influential clan in Bermuda. Obviously his marriage solidified Dinwiddie's position in that outpost of empire.

Did he, undoubtedly brought up as a Presbyterian in Glasgow, become an Anglican in consequence of his marriage? The church records of eighteenth-century Bermuda have been lost, and no answer to that question can be given with assurance. But it is clear enough that he was in later life a champion, if not a communicant, of the Church of England. Dinwiddie acquired at least some of the habits and notions of an English gentleman. He enjoyed convivial imbibing of wine, and was afterward known as a courteous, gracious, and hospitable man.

Dinwiddie was not content to be the head of one of the First Families of Bermuda. His appointments as agent of the admiralty and as customs collector indicate a blossoming ambition for a career in public life. As customs collector he was a decidedly minor British official. The duties performed were not onerous, pay was small, £30 per annum, and he did not even get it until after 1730. But that office gave him increased access to the makers of colonial policy in London, and he used it.

As a merchant and a customs man, Dinwiddie was familiar with the British system of maritime trade regulation. As early as 1731 he submitted information for the improvement of the system to the Board of Trade, an advisory body of officials in London especially responsible for the collection of data and also for the framing of policy concerning the British colonies and overseas commerce and manufacturing. Five years later he reported that the French and the Dutch evaded laws forbidding them to trade with the British colonies in America by fraudulent use of ship papers issued to British colonials. Soon afterward he submitted another document, conveyed to the Board of Trade by Governor Alured Popple of Bermuda, in which he astutely urged the need for establishing a colonial currency—the colonies in America were chronically short of cash.

Very likely he sent information and counsel on other economic and political problems. In 1736 he suggested to the board that a special agent should traverse the American colonies to inspect and report on them, obviously desiring that assignment for himself. Seeking larger fields to conquer, in 1738 he was considering removal to Britain. His application was warmly endorsed by Governor Popple, who had relatives and friends in important places in London.

Indeed, Dinwiddie must have acquired powerful sponsors in England, for he was given in 1738 the post of "Surveyor General of the Southern part of the Continent of North America. viz., South and North Carolina, Virginia, Maryland, Pennsylvania, Bahama Islands and Jamaica." That awkward description of the appointment meant that Horatio Walpole had named Dinwiddie as overseer of the British customs service in a district stretching from Pennsylvania to Jamaica.

The appointment had one drawback. It was most desirable, perhaps even required, that Dinwiddie live in the district. He hoped to have Bermuda included in it, so that he could maintain his residence there; but the Board of Trade declined to give him supervision of Bermuda. Dinwiddie was therefore virtually compelled to leave the islands that had so long been his home in order to accept the appointment. However it was a most dignified post for a man in his situation, and it carried a good salary. He took it.

Precisely how much he received is not known, but he must have been paid more than £300 per annum, the sum received by the poet James Thomson from his less important post as surveyor general of the customs in the Leeward Islands after 1744. The appointment was especially valuable to Dinwiddie in that he held it for life; he could even perform its duties by deputy. It was, in effect, his property. Obviously the Bermuda merchant had become an important figure in the British colonial system. His post had other advantages, because possession of it neither required Dinwiddie to abandon his mercantile enterprises nor precluded another British appointment.

Actually, Dinwiddie probably never spent much effort on the business of his own customs district. Quite possibly in fact, his appointment was in part a reward for undertaking a nasty special assignment as a trusted servant of the crown. For he was immediately sent by the British commissioners of customs to Barbados and the Leeward Islands as an inspector general. They had reason to believe that the collection of a 4½ percent duty on exports from those islands was mishandled. Officers entrusted with that task had long been in the habit of enriching themselves at the expense of the crown.

Dinwiddie sailed to Barbados in 1738; conducted investigations there and in the British Virgin Islands; returned to Bermuda in June 1739 to visit his family; made a hasty visit to Virginia and North Carolina in the summer of that year to look into affairs in his own district; and then sailed to England. He remained in the mother country for many months, submitting at least three reports to the Board of Trade. These included not only his findings concerning the Virgin Islands, but also a disquisition on British territorial rights in the Caribbean Sea and a long and informative essay concerning the population, trade, and value of the British possessions in the New World. He appeared before the board on several occasions to offer more data and further advice on these matters and also on the affairs of Bermuda.

So far as records are concerned, Dinwiddie is then lost to sight for some months. Probably he returned to Bermuda late in 1740 or early in 1741 to wind up his business affairs there —he retained possession of his house in St. George's until his death—and to take his family to Virginia. The Old Dominion lay in the center of his southern customs district. In June 1741 he appeared at Williamsburg. Where he settled cannot absolutely be determined, but he lived forty-six miles from Williamsburg, and most likely he made his home in or near Norfolk. That thriving town made him an honorary citizen, and in return he presented it with a seal. Many Scottish merchants had located there, and Dinwiddie may have visited it earlier in the course of business. Also, several Tuckers, probably relatives of Mrs. Dinwiddie, lived in Norfolk; the surveyor general accepted appointment as godfather of a tiny Tucker.

Dinwiddie, who valued the honors and powers that came to him, immediately became involved in a controversy. As surveyor general he was entitled by his commission to a place on the Council of every colony in his district. Accordingly, in

June 1741 he requested that he be admitted to the Council of Virginia. But membership in that body was also valued by Virginians. Councilors, once appointed, normally served for life. They enjoyed social prestige, and they had easy access to the governor, the font of land grants and other favors. Virginians much preferred a seat in the selected Council to one in the elected House of Burgesses. The advisers of the governor were not eager to admit Dinwiddie into their little circle, and since he was momentarily unable to produce documentary proof of his authority to occupy a place, he was denied one. When that proof became available, he was admitted, on October 15, but not into full membership.

The Council advised the governor, acted as the upper house of the Virginia General Assembly, and was the supreme court of the colony. It was contended, with some reason, that the crown intended Dinwiddie to give his assistance to the governor in executive matters where he could be useful. But he was not invested with legislative or judicial authority, the argument went; he was only a councilor "extraordinary." His fellow councilors declined to accept him as a full-fledged colleague; he insisted that he was, appealed to London, and won the battle. The death of a councilor created a vacancy, and Dinwiddie was formally appointed as a full member in July 1742, and was accepted as such in Williamsburg in April 1743.

But Dinwiddie did not take his oath as "ordinary" councilor until two years more had passed. He did not attend any meeting of the governor's advisors between October 17, 1741, and April 16, 1745. Where was he? He may have remained in Virginia for many months, refusing to serve in the council only as an adviser. He may have traveled about to execute his duties as surveyor general in his own district. He was certainly in London in the early summer of 1743.

One reason for his reappearance in London was that he had spent £1,686—at least so he asserted—in executing his special assignment as inspector general in 1738 and 1739 and that he had been paid only £730. He claimed that he was out of pocket more than £900, and he sought to get the money from the Treasury. He also declared that he had received no pay for his services, and that it had cost him £500 to return to England to petition for redress—he may have suffered losses in business in addition to his traveling expense from Virginia. It is likely that his plea was heeded. Indeed, Dinwiddie was obviously in favor in the chambers of government at Whitehall. Officials were at last acting on the report concerning conditions in Barbados that he had submitted in 1739. Dinwiddie had helped to expose Charles Dunbar, surveyor general of the customs in the southern part of the Caribbean Sea, as an embezzler. Dunbar was discharged. High officers of state sought Dinwiddie's advice. Were there other thieves in the customs service in the West Indies? London showed special concern regarding mismanagement in the collection of the important 4½ per cent duty on exports from Barbados. Dinwiddie appeared at the Treasury in June to suggest ways to improve the customs service there. In August he accepted a second special appointment as inspector general. He agreed to go to Barbados to investigate the collection of the 4½ per cent duty and also to revisit the Leeward Islands to examine the customs service in those sun-drenched colonies. Before he left London he was again consulted about affairs in Bermuda.

Taking a coach from London to Portsmouth, Dinwiddie once more embarked for the Caribbean. Traveling in a British warship, for the War of Jenkins' Ear with Spain was in progress, he arrived at Bridgetown in Barbados in December 1743. Completing his labors there in the following April, he visited Antigua, St. Kitt's, Nevis, and Montserrat, finding ample evidence of thievery among British customs men and using his authority to suspend or dismiss evildoers from office. Dinwiddie suspended Edward Lascelles, Arthur Upton, William Rawlings, and William Eyre, respectively collector, comptroller, and searchers of customs in Barbados. He also discharged Henry Brouncker, the collector on St. Kitt's. Sailing to Virginia in the summer of 1744 to visit his family, he went on to London to report on his activities and to defend his decisions.

Dinwiddie was only too well aware that, doing his duty, he would be attacked in London, especially because Edward Lascelles had an influential brother, Henry, a prominent merchant in London. He took the precaution of appealing for support to Henry Pelham, the prime minister, in a letter sent from Antigua in April 1744. In February 1745 he submitted his final report in person. All of the men he had removed from office complained that they were victims of harsh injustice. However, lengthy investigation by Dinwiddie's superiors led inescapably to the conclusion that all had defrauded the crown.

Softening Dinwiddie's language, the commissioners found the culprits guilty of misconduct rather than fraud. They also chided the inspector general for excessive zeal, and expressed displeasure because he had taken sufficient funds from customs receipts in the islands to pay his expenses—perhaps because he could not readily make use of his own funds. But his triumph was virtually complete, and it was the sweeter because the investigation disclosed that Henry Lascelles, who had preceded his brother as collector of customs in Barbados, had also been guilty of misconduct in that office.

Dinwiddie must have done more voyaging than some British admirals of his time. While the embezzlers were still striving to secure reversal of his decisions, he set off for Virginia. On April 16, 1745, he finally took his oath of office as a full member of the Virginia Council, and he attended meetings of that body until the following September—but reappeared in London in 1746. Doubtless he felt it prudent to be in the city to defend his record against continuing attacks by the Lascelles brothers.

Dinwiddie established himself and his family in London and engaged in business there for about five years. He invested in ships, was a major partner with his brother Lawrence in a factory in Glasgow that produced delft pottery, and continued to prosper. Had he become tired of public office? Not wishing to return to Virginia to do duty as surveyor general, he consigned that post, in 1749, to Peter Randolph of Virginia. How much Randolph paid him for it is not known. When Dinwiddie declared that he intended to remain in London he was removed from the Council of Virginia, since a councilor had to reside in the colony where he held office. It seemed that his official and direct connection with the Old Dominion was permanently severed.

But if desire for public preferment and social advance waned in Dinwiddie, it soon revived. The resignation that same year of Sir William Gooch, lieutenant governor of Virginia, ultimately opened a most attractive prospect to the Lon-

don merchant. He sought to succeed Gooch. His performance as a public servant in the colonies and his familiarity with their problems did not hurt his chances. In the spring of 1750 and again in the early months of 1751 he testified as an expert on colonial questions in Parliament.

Always active in cultivating acquaintances who might be useful to him, Dinwiddie had established connections with various influential and powerful persons in London: he had gained the friendship of John Hanbury, a wealthy merchant engaged in trade to the Chesapeake; more important, he was favorably known to Henry Pelham, the prime minister; he had the support of Horatio Walpole, a close political ally of Pelham; he had also somehow won the good will of John Carteret, Earl Granville, who became president of the Privy Council in June of that year; and he had secured the friendship of George Dunk, earl of Halifax, president of the Board of Trade and chief architect of British colonial policy after 1748.

Dinwiddie saw America exactly as Halifax did. Afterward known in England as "Father of the Colonies," Halifax was actually a most determined defender of the authority of Britain over her territories beyond the Atlantic. And so was Dinwiddie, whose appointment as lieutenant governor of Virginia was made official on July 4, 1751, precisely a quarter of a century before the Americans asserted their independence from Britain. He was once—because of patronage he extended to George Washington—called "Grandfather of the American Revolution." But he was not, and he never became, a champion of American rights.

It is necessary to remember that Dinwiddie did not become the titular governor of Virginia; his official title was lieutenant governor. But he was the chief executive in reality; and the Virginia practice of referring to Dinwiddie as governor is so convenient that it is adopted in this volume. The official title of governor was held by William Anne Keppel, earl of Albemarle, courtier, wastrel, favorite of King George II, and British ambassador to France. The governorship of Virginia at that time was a political plum in London, and Dinwiddie had to share with Albemarle the salary and perquisites of the office.

So eager was Dinwiddie to go to Williamsburg that he agreed to pay Albemarle no less than £3,300 per annum, in theory one half the income attached to the governorship. But that does not mean Dinwiddie received an equal sum as lieutenant governor. His annual salary was only £2,000; he collected substantial fees, but they can hardly have amounted to so much as £4,600 per year. Clearly Albemarle squeezed as much money as possible out of Dinwiddie, and the lieutenant governor learned to regret that he had entered into an agreement so favorable to the British courtier. To be sure, Dinwiddie not only had private means that guaranteed him a comfortable living, but he received the use of a house in Williamsburg, and gained an opportunity to increase the fees collected by the acting executive of the Old Dominion.

Chapter 2
Defender of the Faith

Robert Dinwiddie's predecessor, Sir William Gooch, served for twenty-two years in Williamsburg and retained the affection of many Virginians to the very end of his tenure. Ordinarily, however, the Americans cordially welcomed a royal governor and were more pleased by his departure. If he defended the authority of Britain against the colonists— and it was his duty to do so—he almost invariably incurred the enmity of colonials seeking power for themselves and freedom from British domination. A tactful man might soften such clashes; a less scrupulous or lazy one might please local politicians by neglecting to execute detailed instructions supplied to every governor by his superiors in London.

Dinwiddie was devoted to duty. He sedulously obeyed orders from London. He kept up his contacts with influential men in England, such as the earl of Halifax, Horatio Walpole, and Earl Granville, not only for his own interests but for those of the Virginians—as he saw those interests. Sensible, industrious, friendly, and hospitable, he did all that he could— given his loyalty to duty and to Britain—to please the people of the Old Dominion. But he was also ambitious and unfortunate.

There can be no question that the new governor, despite mounting troubles, enjoyed his powers and prestige for many months. He liked the Virginia climate. "The air is temperate," he wrote, "the extreme heat in summer, or cold in winter is but of short duration, as they are frequently relieved with intervening cold and warm breezes."

When the earl of Albemarle died in Paris late in 1754, Dinwiddie's situation in Williamsburg became precarious. He could not hope to succeed Albemarle. He could and did hope that the British ministry would leave the titular governorship vacant for "a few years," during which he could enjoy all of the salary and fees paid to the governor. Such an arrangement would repay him in part for "the great expences" he had incurred. But he feared that many British noblemen would covet the handsome sinecure, and that one of them would soon obtain it. In that case, Dinwiddie could do no more than try to make a bargain with the new titular governor like the one he had entered into with Albemarle.

By May 1755 Dinwiddie learned that he might even lose his appointment in Williamsburg. Some men in high place in London believed it desirable not merely to select a British nobleman to replace Albemarle, but to choose one who would cross the Atlantic and serve in Williamsburg. Such an arrangement, they thought, would flatter the Virginians and attach them more firmly to the mother country. No fewer than four lords were considered for the post. But no man of high rank thought it worth his while to serve in Virginia for £2,000 per year and valuable perquisites. Such men eagerly begged for pensions and for appointments to which no work was attached; except for munificent rewards they would not exchange the amenities and fleshpots of Britain and the European continent for troubles with uncouth colonists and savage Indians.

After much delay the ministry at last chose another absentee governor. In 1756 General John Campbell, earl of Loudoun, newly named commander in chief of the British army in North America, was put in the place of Albemarle. Dinwiddie continued to serve in Williamsburg, sending to Loudoun the sums each year that he had hitherto paid to Albemarle. By that time the agonies of office were at least equal to its pleasures for him.

Immediately after their arrival in Williamsburg the Dinwiddies were wined and dined by several of the principal families in the town: Mr. and Mrs. Peyton Randolph, Mr. and Mrs. John Blair, Dr. and Mrs. George Gilmer, Dr. and Mrs. Peter Hay. They were sufficiently established to entertain guests in their own home the day after Christmas. Because the Governor's Palace was being repaired, the Dinwiddies occupied the Robert Carter House for about a year.

Thereafter they inhabited the splendidly renovated Palace and lived in appropriate state. The governor maintained a coach. He brought silver from England, and he bought a half-dozen or more Negro slaves to perform household chores. Among the family possessions was a harpsichord, on which Elizabeth and Rebecca probably practiced, which, perhaps, Mrs. Dinwiddie played. The Dinwiddies were generously hospitable, polite, and truly amiable. The enemies he made, even the most passionate of them, did not accuse him of mean thrift or bad manners.

The Dinwiddies were hosts to British generals and naval officers, governors of American colonies, travelers without office, and even Cherokee Indian chiefs—as well as Virginia friends. They entertained elegantly at the Palace and gave a ball to celebrate the birthday of George II in November. The governor, despite his gloomy Glasgow background, was by no means a killjoy.

During his lifetime it was illegal to offer plays in Glasgow. Perhaps for this reason, when a company of traveling English actors from London appeared in Williamsburg, in 1752, Dinwiddie and his council at first decided to refuse them permission to perform in the town. But the governor and his advisers sensibly changed their minds. Accordingly, the players, headed by Lewis Hallam, presented *The Merchant of Venice* and *The Anatomist* in September of that year and continued to give performances until the summer of 1753. Perhaps the most interesting of all their portrayals occurred on November 4, when they offered *Othello* and a pantomime in which actors wielded naked swords. In the audience were the "Emperor" and "Empress" of the Cherokee nation with their son. The wife of the Indian chief urged that the players be separated to prevent murder.

The governor demonstrated in other ways that he was a civilized man. He gave some books to the College of William and Mary, and he contributed generously to the support of a student, John Esten, at that institution. When Lieutenant John Gray of South Carolina, in distress, asked Dinwiddie for public money that had not been voted to him, the governor gave Gray £25 from his own pocket.

All this does not mean that a paragon entered the renovated

Palace. Dinwiddie was a friendly man but he had a temper, which he displayed on occasion. Not an imposing proconsul, he was a successful merchant and customs man, too old to acquire the guise and all the graces of a governing aristocrat. He could not please or awe Virginia gentlemen and ladies who were disposed to love nobles, who would have been delighted had the profligate Albemarle been the first citizen of Williamsburg and Virginia, and who were afterward glad to have Lord Botetourt in their Palace. His language was homely and unsophisticated. It was beyond his power to turn a fetching phrase to impress members of a House of Burgesses disposed to find fault. His speeches to that body were much less than inspiring; humorless, moralistic, and chauvinistic, they appeal now only because of their brevity.

Virginians saw in their governor's chair a stocky Scot tending to corpulence, neither handsome nor homely, masculine, sturdy, intelligent: a blue-eyed, red-faced, double-chinned man who had enjoyed food and wine. The more observing might notice that the new governor's eyes were sharp. He would demonstrate anew in Williamsburg the intelligence and energy that had enabled him to climb so far in the world. But he did not become a broadminded statesman who could see Virginia and America as did the Virginians and Americans. He remained utterly British in viewpoint.

But Dinwiddie, within his British limits, did indeed seek to please the Virginians, and the House of Burgesses at first responded. He soon called that body into session, and it unanimously voted him a present of £500, ostensibly to reimburse him for the expenses he incurred on his journey from England to Virginia, but actually, at least in part, to encourage him to support the lawmakers of the Old Dominion against defenders of the royal prerogative in London. The burgesses also consented to the organization of a new county named after the governor.

But Dinwiddie just as quickly discovered that it was difficult to satisfy both the Virginians and his superiors in London. Both could be, and often were, unreasonable. Thus, he received orders from London in 1753 to send £1,000 from funds voted by the Virginia assembly for Virginia purposes to the governor of South Carolina, so that he might buy presents for Indians, presumably to the benefit of the British empire. That order obviously and flagrantly flouted the long-recognized right of the assembly to designate the purposes for which Virginia tax receipts could be spent. Dinwiddie obeyed. He and his Council strove to avert a protest from the House of Burgesses. Temporarily keeping the affair a secret in Williamsburg, they sent a strong protest to London, asking, to no avail, that the British Treasury reimburse the Old Dominion. The crown's insistence on taking Virginia money without Virginia consent gave the burgesses good reason to inveigh against royal usurpation.

However, the burgesses' own behavior with respect to public money was not beyond reproach. Early in 1754 Dinwiddie begged them to check advances by the French in the upper valley of the Ohio River. Were they still angry because London had arbitrarily spent £1,000 of their tax receipts? They voted money, but they tried to place control over its expenditure in a committee of their own members. Such an arrangement—not unprecedented in Virginia—infringed upon the executive power of the governor. "The people here are too much bent on a republican spirit," complained Dinwiddie. To get the money, he was finally forced to accept a system by which his outlays from that money were approved by a joint committee of the House of Burgesses and the Council.

Thereafter the lower house successfully insisted, until 1757, that the same system be employed in the spending of all sums it voted for defense. The result was that John Robinson, speaker of the House of Burgesses, treasurer of Virginia, and principal member of all such committees, gained great power —Dinwiddie had to account to Robinson for all his expenditures out of those funds. Besides, Robinson used his influence over the burgesses and his authority over money to assert his will in other matters that were obviously executive in their nature.

These nasty squabbles over money and power embittered the famous controversy between Dinwiddie and the burgesses over the pistole fee—the pistole was not a weapon but a Spanish coin worth about four-fifths of the British pound. That struggle—of which more later—was also exacerbated by, even arose in some part from, a contest over the presidency of the College of William and Mary and other local offices between two Anglican clergymen, brothers-in-law.

If Dinwiddie was not an Anglican communicant, he undoubtedly occupied the pew reserved for the governor in the Bruton Parish Church at Williamsburg. Moreover, and beyond any question, he asserted his influence in behalf of the Anglican establishment in Virginia. No believer in religious freedom, he was a forthright enemy of the Roman Catholic church and referred to its priests in Maryland as "vermin who are a pest to society." They ought, he said, to be "expunged" by law.

In his first years of office he was not kind to Presbyterians either, although his sister Janet, "an uncommonly judicious, pious woman," had married one. Her husband, the Reverend William McCulloch, was a very close friend of the Reverend George Whitefield, the great revivalist. At Cambuslang, near Glasgow, where McCulloch was pastor, McCulloch and Whitefield once exhorted an enormous crowd to give themselves to the Lord. Whitefield rejoiced when he learned that Dinwiddie had succeeded Gooch. He believed, wrongly, that Gooch had been utterly hostile to enthusiastic evangelists. "I, therefore, think Mr. Dinwiddie is raised up to succeed him, in order to befriend the Church of God, and the interest of Christ's people."

As a matter of fact, the governor encouraged neither Presbyterian nor Anglican enthusiasts. The distinguished Reverend Samuel Davies, principal founder of the Presbyterian church in Virginia and a most successful proselyter for it in the middle of the eighteenth century, aroused his ire. Davies, like Anglican clergymen, was required by Virginia law to confine his activities to one parish. He disobeyed the law, preaching in seven meeting houses scattered over five counties. He even sought from Dinwiddie a license that would permit him to offer the Presbyterian word of God to an eighth congregation.

After talking to Davies, the governor reached the interesting and surely erroneous conclusion that the preacher—afterward briefly the president of Princeton—was moved by "a lucrative view" rather than by desire for "the salvation of the people." He peremptorily informed Davies that he was not free to preach whenever he wished, that seven meeting houses were more than enough for one clergyman. He permitted Davies to employ an assistant.

But the governor could not prevent the spread of Presbyterianism in Virginia, nor was he eager to act against the church of his childhood. He learned to respect Davies and later recommended him to Lawrence Dinwiddie and to William and Janet McCulloch. In consequence, they hospitably entertained Davies at Glasgow and Cambuslang in July 1754, when he visited Britain on religious and educational business. After talking to William McCulloch about discrimination against Dissenters in Virginia, Davies recorded in his diary, "I have reason to believe that Governor Dinwiddie would favour them were it not so opposite to his interest."

Davies returned to Virginia in February 1755 with a legal opinion that the English Act of Toleration of 1689, which permitted Dissenters to preach without reference to parish boundaries, applied to Virginia and that the Virginia law which cramped his activities was therefore void. Immediately after landing he went to Williamsburg and conferred with the governor. It is not recorded that Dinwiddie afterward went to hear Davies preach or that he welcomed George Whitefield when that great evangelist came to Virginia. But the governor had been given good reason to refrain from efforts to limit the activities of Presbyterians and other Dissenters, and he ceased to disturb them.

An enemy of Dinwiddie, who remains unknown, would have it that the governor was still a Presbyterian, at least at heart. He put the following verses in Dinwiddie's mouth:

> I'm Fidei deputy defensor *
> And to the end of my Vice reign
> Must orthodox opinions feign,
> Tho' I still think, as at first taught,
> Out of the Kirks pale all was naught,
> That each law slieve and Mitred head
> Will surely to perdition lead.
> I wish their necks were in a halter,
> My principles will never alter.

* That is, defender of the Anglican faith, as lieutenant governor.

Robert Dinwiddie, artist unidentified. Courtesy of the National Portrait Gallery, London

The Dinwiddie Sisters, a portrait of the governor's daughters, Rebecca and Elizabeth, by Allan Ramsay. Courtesy of the Trustees of the Lady Lever Art Gallery, Port Sunlight, Cheshire.

However, Dinwiddie not only defended the official church of the colony, but asserted the rights of the crown and of the Anglican clergy against the laymen of the vestries. The latter sought the power to hire and fire their parish clergymen, and they were not without friends in the House of Burgesses. The governor, who headed the established church in Virginia in the same fashion that George II headed it in England, insisted that he should normally appoint and dismiss clergymen recommended by the bishop of London—that dignitary being directly responsible for the welfare of the Anglican church in the colonies—and by the bishop's commissary in Virginia. But the vestry of Lunenburg Parish did not hesitate to drive the Reverend William Kay from its church without consulting Dinwiddie or any superior Anglican authority.

The governor stirred up far more trouble for himself by favoring the Reverend Thomas Dawson of Bruton Parish Church in Williamsburg against the Reverend William Stith, whose Henrico parish was at some distance from the capital. Dawson had entertained the new governor soon after his arrival, and the Dawsons and Dinwiddies became intimate friends. When the Reverend William Dawson, older brother of Thomas, commissary of the bishop of London in Virginia, president of the College of William and Mary, and member of the Council, died in 1752, Dinwiddie strove to secure his several offices for Thomas and precipitated a clash that had unexpected and most untoward consequences for the governor.

For Stith, author of a history of Virginia, would not permit the honors and salaries attached to those offices to go to his brother-in-law—Thomas Dawson had married his sister—without a struggle. Stith, like his brother-in-law, was a graduate of Queen's College, Oxford; and he had earlier taught in the grammar school at William and Mary. In asserting his claims to preferment he had the support of the numerous Randolph clan, to which he was related through his mother. Stith doubtless also gained adherents who saw Thomas Dawson as a member of a closed ring of Williamsburg favorites. In August the Board of Visitors of the college, by a majority of nine to eight with Dinwiddie voting in the minority, named Stith as the new president of William and Mary.

A hotheaded and quarrelsome man, Stith was not content with his campus victory. He became an ardent enemy of Dinwiddie; and the defeated governor developed no affection for the aggressive historian. So long as Dinwiddie presided over the Council, Stith could not hope to secure William Dawson's seat in that body. But he dared to believe that, despite the hostility of the governor, he could get William Dawson's post as commissary of the bishop of London. He applied to the bishop. He pointed out that the man who presided over the College of William and Mary usually also served as commissary over the Anglican clergy in Virginia.

The bishop, the old and ailing Thomas Sherlock, denied the post to Stith. The bishop had received an application from Thomas Dawson too, and it was ardently supported by Dinwiddie and John Blair, a respected member of the council and a pillar of the established church in Virginia. Dinwiddie and Blair praised Thomas Dawson and condemned Stith; Blair said that Stith was unstable and hinted that he was heretical; both Blair and Dinwiddie denounced him as an enemy of order in Virginia; Dinwiddie asserted that Stith stirred up the "lower class of people" against the governor, that he tried "to sow sedition." The bishop not only gave the appointment to Thomas Dawson, but scolded the historian for his impudence.

Befriended by Dinwiddie, Thomas Dawson ultimately won almost complete victory over his brother-in-law. When Stith died in 1755, after enjoying the presidency of William and Mary for only three years, Dawson succeeded to that post. He also entered the Council on the recommendation of Dinwiddie, for the governor continued to respect him and to like him. Let it not be thought, however, that Dawson was utterly saintly; after Dinwiddie's departure from Williamsburg Dawson was forced to apologize to its citizens for being drunk in public.

But Dinwiddie could not derive complete satisfaction from the outcome of his struggles with Stith. For that clergyman was a principal assailant of the governor in the harassing contest over the pistole fee. Hence Dinwiddie's unwarranted charge that Stith was guilty of "sedition." Dinwiddie was angry because Stith and leaders of the House of Burgesses assailed him, not without success, as a grasping champion of arbitrary rule who sought illegally to fill his own pockets at the expense of worthy and abused Virginians.

The governor did learn to avoid religious pitfalls. In the fall of 1755 a new issue arose that eventually erupted into a nasty struggle almost as bruising as that over the pistole fee. As a steady friend of the Anglican clergy he was urged to veto a bill presented by the burgesses which temporarily authorized the payment of the clergymen in cash rather than in tobacco—the men of the cloth had been compensated in tobacco but its price had risen high. Dinwiddie hesitated. John Robinson assured him that a veto must lead to another fight. Commissary Thomas Dawson, solicitous for the welfare of the clergy under his direction but eager to preserve the public peace, also urged the governor not to stand against the will of the burgesses.

Dinwiddie prudently signed the measure. He did not encourage the clergy to contend for higher pay at the expense of their parishioners; nor did he challenge the burgesses in behalf of the rectors. He was in no way responsible for the clash that soon afterward developed over the issue of clerical pay and that led to the divisive Parson's Cause. It is much to his credit that Dinwiddie earned the esteem, if not the affection, of the Reverend Samuel Davies before he abandoned the governorship. After news came to Virginia that Dinwiddie had reached England, Davies said, "I rejoice to hear that our former governor is safe arrived in his native country once more. May the evening of his life be calm & bright."

Chapter 3
Challenge from the Burgesses

Afterward Dinwiddie must have wished many times that he had never heard the word *pistole*. But he had not become prosperous by neglecting opportunities to make money, and he sought to acquire as much cash as he legitimately could from the governorship. Despite the large payments he made to the earl of Albemarle, the office apparently gave him a substantial income; he tried to add to it.

In every one of the royal colonies in North America except Virginia the governor was permitted the charge for affixing an official seal to a patent for land. Before Dinwiddie left London to assume his duties as the head of state in Williamsburg, he asked that he be authorized to exact similar payments in Virginia, or that the Council of the colony be instructed to require them. The London government did not respond to this request before he departed for America—British officials of that time were remarkable neither for efficiency nor for rapid action. However, he may have been given informal assurance that his proposal was acceptable. Perhaps someone in authority told him that special action was unnecessary, since the instructions supplied to all royal governors in America asserted that they could establish fees with the consent of their councils. In any event, in April 1752 the Virginia Council gave its consent to a fee of one pistole, payable to the governor each time he affixed his seal.

The pistole was no great sum of money. Afterward Dinwiddie said that collection of the fee would bring him only a "trifling income." He did not need the revenue; as indicated earlier, his private fortune was substantial and his salary, coupled with other fees, supplied him with sufficient funds to live graciously in Williamsburg. He was lending money to various Virginians. Nor was a pistole in itself a great matter to those Virginians who obtained grants of land, usually in large quantities, from the governor and his Council.

But Dinwiddie also insisted that land grants be promptly patented, and the owners of patented lands were compelled by law to pay quitrents. Thus he aroused the ire of many influential Virginians, including members of the House of Burgesses. They had long been able to secure handsome grants of land in the interior of the colony at little expense and to keep them until the westward advance of settlers enhanced the value of their holdings. They had been required only to have their tracts surveyed. So they had been excused over long periods of time from paying quitrents. The fee that Dinwiddie sought was small; but his demand that patenting promptly follow surveying was not a trifling matter.

Dinwiddie's new policy with respect to land grants must in any case have stimulated hostility among Virginia speculators. Their resentment was fanned to fury by William Stith, who was chaplain of the House of Burgesses as well as president of the College of William and Mary after the summer of 1752. Stith denounced the pistole fee in public and in private as exorbitant—it was lower than similar charges in other colonies—and as illegal. He offered a toast at table in his home, "Liberty Property & No Pistole." That toast became a slogan for outraged land speculators.

Stith did not hesitate to assail Dinwiddie in a letter to Bishop Sherlock, a dignitary whom he could not expect to turn against the governor. Stith said that Dinwiddie demanded the fee "after he had received all the presents from the country which he could at that time hope for or expect"; that exaction of it was "against Law"; that the fee was "subversive of the rights and liberties of my country"; and that "he would have made us a good governor, had he not been unhappily led into this wrong step which hath raised so great a disaffection in the people, and caused so general a distrust of him."

Unfortunately for Dinwiddie, Stith gained the ardent support of the controlling faction in the House of Burgesses led by planter John Robinson, a faction that included members of the Randolph clan. Dinwiddie could rely on a majority of the councilors, among them Thomas Nelson of Yorktown and Colonel Richard Corbin (who were, like Dinwiddie, connected by marriage with the Tuckers) William Nelson, a brother of Thomas, and John Blair.

At an earlier time he might have obtained help among the burgesses from a party, led by Colonel Thomas Lee, that had struggled for mastery with the Robinson-Randolph clique; but Colonel Lee was dead and his numerous sons, afterward so potent in Virginian and American politics, had not yet come to the fore. The governor was confronted by a solid phalanx of adversaries in the House of Burgesses. Even the attorney general of the colony, Peyton Randolph, turned against him.

The burgesses were not only firmly but passionately against the fee. It was in itself most obnoxious, especially to members who held or hoped to hold lands without paying quitrents. Worse yet, it appeared to be an arbitrary exaction by executive fiat, less to be tolerated because for many decades all fees had been established by the Virginia Assembly. Burgesses could remember that moneys had been taken from Virginia tax receipts and sent to South Carolina by order from London. The pistole fee became an enormous grievance in the minds of men in the lower house. If its collection were permitted, would not the governor demand other new fees? And was there any real difference between the imposition of heavy and numerous fees and the levying of taxes? Members of the House became enraged, as angry as the Reverend William Stith.

Confronted by mounting animosity among the burgesses, Dinwiddie again sought reinforcement from London for his right to collect the pistole fee. In October 1752 he asked the Board of Trade for its consent. That body responded with unusual celerity, approving the fee in January 1753. Moreover, in the following month Sir Dudley Rider, attorney general and solicitor general for the crown, asserted in a formal opinion that the governor and Council of Virginia unquestionably possessed power to establish the fee.

Many hundreds of Virginians who held land by survey only now applied for patents in accordance with the demand of the governor. But if he fancied that the Old Dominion would yield to imperial authority, he erred sadly. Richard Bland, prominent member of the House of Burgesses, published in 1753 an essay that denounced the fee as illegal and hinted that it was also unconstitutional, on the ground that it violated the rights of Englishmen. When the burgesses convened in the fall of that year, they received petitions against the fee from six counties.

The burgesses, however, needed no prodding from their constituents. The lower house urged Dinwiddie to abandon his effort to collect the pistole. The fee was illegal, they asserted; besides, it would discourage people from taking up and settling lands in western Virginia, thus hindering growth of the colony. The burgesses pointed out that one of his predecessors in office, Lord Howard of Effingham, had tried to exact such a fee late in the seventeenth century, and that the British Privy Council had ordered Howard to abandon his efforts to collect it.

Dinwiddie insisted on his right to demand the pistole and made it clear to the burgesses that he had received the blessing of authorities in London. He said that its collection was necessary in order to force the Virginians to pay their quitrents. Thereupon, in December, the burgesses forthrightly challenged the governor. Acting in secrecy—to make sure that he would not dismiss them before they could accomplish their purposes—they condemned the fee as unconstitutional, decided to appeal to London, and declared that anyone who paid the pistole was "a betrayer" of "the rights and privileges of the people."

The House of Burgesses rejected a compromise offered by the Council, a proposal that the two houses unite to pass a law establishing the fee. The burgesses would not sanction the charge, legal or illegal, constitutional or unconstitutional; and their pronouncement that anyone who paid it was a "betrayer" of his country prevented less courageous and more cautious citizens from giving Dinwiddie his pistole. He offered to give patents to men who had had their lands surveyed in the past without the fee, if those men would pay quitrents from the time of survey. They refused his offer. Petitions for patents piled up in his office.

So determined were the burgesses to thwart Dinwiddie that they resorted to extraordinary measures to assure forceful presentation of their case in London. They sent Peyton Randolph, one of their own members but also royal attorney general, across the ocean to represent them. They offered him £2,500 Virginia money for his services. Besides, if Dinwiddie discharged him from his post as attorney general, they promised him a pension of £300 for life.

These measures were taken without the consent of Dinwiddie or the Council. Moreover, John Robinson, treasurer of the colony as well as speaker of the House of Burgesses, declared that Randolph would be paid from public funds whether or not the governor and Council gave their consent. The governor urged Randolph not to accept the appointment, pointing out that it was inconsistent with Randolph's duty as a royal officer. Randolph refused to listen to the governor. Dinwiddie then declared the office of attorney general vacant and gave George Wythe a temporary appointment to it. He asked officials in England to support him against the burgesses, and he employed his friend in London, James Abercromby, to plead his case against Randolph.

Challenging British authority, the burgesses could not reasonably hope to win a complete victory in London. Peyton Randolph executed his mission with energy. He sought to win friends and influence office holders. He attacked Dinwiddie in a London newspaper, and he undoubtedly helped secure publication there early in 1754 of a pamphlet by his fellow burgess, Landon Carter, in which Carter vigorously defended the actions of the lower house. Dinwiddie was informed that his Virginia opponents even tried to enlist the help of Dinwiddie's old enemy, Henry Lascelles. If so, they labored in vain, for Lascelles died in October 1753. But Abercromby also solicited favor assiduously in behalf of Dinwiddie, and Lord Halifax, always a champion of the authority of Britain over the colonies, came forth as the protector of the governor.

By the spring of 1754 Dinwiddie deeply regretted that he

had asked for the pistoles. He informed Abercromby that he would not demand fees for probating wills or for authenticating the appointment of executors of estates in Virginia. He had learned that the earl of Halifax would defend him, but that Halifax was "Chagreen'd" because the governor had permitted himself to become involved in such a nasty dispute.

The complaint against Dinwiddie came before the Privy Council in June 1754. Peyton Randolph employed two prominent lawyers, Robert Henley and Alexander Forrester, to represent the burgesses. Abercromby obtained the services of William Murray, afterward renowned as Lord Mansfield, and Alexander Hume Campbell, two Scots who overcame their opponents in legal knowledge and astutely appealed to the prejudices of the members of the Privy Council.

Murray and Campbell insisted that grasping land speculators inspired the burgesses to oppose Dinwiddie. Murray declared that Peyton Randolph had been granted four hundred thousand acres and that he had never paid a penny for them. Murray and Campbell would have it that the crown owned all ungranted lands in Virginia; that the crown could permit Dinwiddie to impose any charge, however great, in connection with the disposal of such lands; that it had approved the pistole fee; and that the fee was moderate. They declared that Dinwiddie was willing to accept, in lieu of it, payments proportioned to the size of land grants. They scoffed at the claim that precedent was against Dinwiddie. True, Lord Howard, attempting to make such a charge, had been rebuked by his superiors in London—but on the ground that he had not secured the consent of his Council. Anyway, regardless of the Lord Howard affair, regardless of Virginia practice, the power of the crown over land grants was undiminished. Campbell was irked that it should be challenged by a "puny House of Burgesses" that "boldly dared to do, what the House of Commons in England never presumed to attempt." Murray and Campbell asserted that the burgesses, authorizing the expenditure of Virginia money without the consent of the Council and the governor, were indeed usurpers of power.

Henley and Forrester put the case for the burgesses as best they could. They accused Dinwiddie of "avarice"; contended that the Lord Howard affair did offer precedent; argued that

Dinwiddie, as a mere lieutenant governor, had less standing than Howard; that long practice favored the contentions of the burgesses; that Virginians obtaining large grants of land did not reap huge profits therefrom; and that persons seeking to get smaller quantities of land could not afford to pay the pistole.

The Privy Council quickly reached its decision. The right of the governor to demand a fee was upheld. He was instructed to collect it only on patents of one hundred acres or more lying east of the Allegheny Mountains; and the fee was not to be retroactive. Nor was he to demand it on patents of lands lying beyond the mountains. Settlement in the Mississippi Valley was to be encouraged. However, no person was to be granted more than one thousand acres in the regions west of the mountains. The Privy Council both upheld Dinwiddie and struck at Virginia land speculators.

But the governor had won a battle, not the war. His superiors had not supported him in his efforts to force prompt payment of quitrents. He prudently abandoned his attempts —it was now their responsibility to compel the obedience of the Virginians—he had made more than enough enemies by trying to do his duty. Moreover, he was plagued by questions concerning Peyton Randolph. He called the burgesses together in August 1754, and asked them to vote money for defense against the French.

The burgesses passed a bill to supply £20,000—and then added to it a "rider" authorizing the payment to Randolph of the £2,500 they had promised him. Dinwiddie urged the house to set aside the rider, but it refused. He could not have the money for defense unless he authorized payment of Randolph. So eager was he to secure the £20,000 that he offered to sign a separate bill, subject to approval in London, to give Randolph his £2,500. But that proposal did not satisfy the burgesses. He must accept the rider or manage without the money for defense.

Dinwiddie, with the support of his Council, would not yield to the demand of the burgesses, "this stubborn generation"; he sent them home. In the fall of 1754 the governor learned that Randolph had failed in his mission to London. But he also received from the Board of Trade a recommendation, a "very disagreeable" one, that he consider restoring Randolph to his office of attorney general. The board was obviously trying to put an end to the dispute over the pistole fee.

It has been observed that Dinwiddie sought honors as well as money. On December 20, 1754, the University of Glasgow, having conferred upon him the degree of Master of Arts twenty-six years earlier while he was a resident of Bermuda, now gave him the title of Doctor of Laws. The citation unanimously endorsed by the faculty members of his alma mater declared with unusual bluntness that the degree was awarded because Dinwiddie, a native of Glasgow and an alumnus of the university, "by the high office he bears does honour to both, and may have occasion to promote their interest." Nevertheless, the governor was more deserving of his new academic title than many who have received it. In the fall of 1754 and the winter that followed, he demonstrated that he was not without political acumen.

Even though he continued to believe that the authority of Britain over her colonies in America must be vigorously asserted, the governor still had to try to settle somehow his quarrel with the House of Burgesses in general and with Peyton Randolph in particular. An accommodation was necessary if for no other reason than to secure money from the lower house to raise and send military forces against the French in the upper part of the Ohio Valley. How might he persuade the burgesses, who could not be much pleased by the result of their campaign against him in London, to vote that money? His problem was the more difficult because of word he received from London even before he learned the outcome of the struggle in that city over the pistole fee. George II, responding to pleas for help from the governor, was sending him £10,000 in cash, plus a credit for another £10,000, to be spent in the struggle against the French.

On the surface, the action taken by His Majesty seemed to be a generous one. But there was a catch in it. For the powers in London stipulated that the £20,000 be repaid to the crown out of receipts from the Virginia export tax on tobacco levied by the assembly. The British ministry proposed, in effect, to spend Virginia tax money for military purposes, in precisely the same fashion that it had ordered such money sent to South Carolina in 1753 to purchase presents for the Indians. Another such usurpation—and for a far larger sum—must arouse keen resentment among the burgesses.

The governor unhappily contemplated the situation. He had become so tired of the conflict with them that he had proposed that Parliament pass an act to compel the Virginians —and other American colonists—to obey the king's commands and to provide for their own defense. He wrote to Governor Horatio Sharpe, who had his own troubles as chief executive of Maryland:

A governor in the discharge of his duty to his King & Country, is much to be pitied, when it's considered his transactions with an obstinate assembly; full of their own opinions & entirely deaf to arguments & reason; I assure you I am heartily fatigued & quite weary with the unjust opposition to every thing proposed to them for the genl. good.

Dinwiddie still felt the sting of personal abuse, too. One of his enemies wrote:

When skill in barter lent you wings
To reach the virgin shore
Small favour from the best of kings
With you was wafted o'er.

You promis'd to relieve our woes,
And with great kindness treat us;
But whorf; awaw! each infant knows
Your whole design's to eat us.

Of wiley snares, to trap the foes,
Or of his blood a spiller,
You guiltless are, & will be so,
Your whole concern's the siller.

However, assisted by his Council, Dinwiddie found a way to avoid struggle over the £20,000 for the time being, and even to make use of the royal grant in negotiations with the House of Burgesses. He kept secret the fact that Virginia was ordered to repay the money. Writing home to officials and to influential friends, he again urged that the British ministry refrain, at least temporarily, from requiring a raid on

Virginia revenues. Calling the burgesses into session in October, he informed them that their king had generously provided the £20,000, together with weapons, for operations against the detested French. Inveighing against the French—those foreign enemies who would, if they could, impose a "yoak of civil and religious slavery" on the English colonists in America—he urged the burgesses to do their share to preserve freedom for themselves and their progeny. Surely they would now supply the £20,000 they had earlier refused to vote without a clogging amendment in behalf of Peyton Randolph.

The immediate response of the burgesses, prepared by Landon Carter, was not very encouraging. The governor was tartly informed that "the welfare of our Country" was "the only governing motive in all our resolutions, however illy they have been represented." But the burgesses were now willing to make a small concession. They offered Dinwiddie a bargain—payment of Randolph in a bill to be approved by the governor and Council as well as the House of Burgesses; appropriation of £20,000 for defense, with expenditures from it to be approved by the joint committee of burgesses and councilors controlled by Robinson.

The governor prudently accepted the bargain, made the less distasteful to him because John Robinson personally expressed his regret that the burgesses had been rude to Dinwiddie. "I think we are now on a very good footing, which I desire may long continue, and surely it will be all their own faults if it does not, as I shall now do everything in my power to establish it, agreeable to instructions," he wrote. In January, 1755 Dinwiddie appointed Thomas Stevens to be inspector at Mantapike to please Robinson. In August of that year he declared that he lived "in great harmony" with the Virginians. But the enmity aroused by his effort to increase his perquisites persisted; and other issues remained and developed that rendered full concord between him and the burgesses impossible.

There still remained for Dinwiddie a question arising from the fight over the pistole fee: What to do about the recommendation from London that he consider the restoration of Peyton Randolph to his office as attorney general? The governor, who believed that Randolph had wantonly abused him in London, was very reluctant to forgive him. But Dinwiddie could hardly refuse to execute the recommendation of Lord Halifax and the Board of Trade. The earl of Albemarle settled the matter. There was some danger that the quarrel over the pistole fee might disturb Albemarle's sinecure appointment as titular governor. He therefore urged the lieutenant governor to restore Randolph to office.

Dinwiddie had no real choice left, but he was able to yield with dignity. The Randolph who returned to Virginia was much less obstreperous than the Randolph who went to London to assail Dinwiddie. He did not know that the governor was under extreme pressure to restore him to his office. Dinwiddie forced him to apologize in writing for at least parts of his conduct, to promise to do his duty as attorney general, and to pledge himself to show proper respect for Dinwiddie in return for renewal of his appointment. Only then did Dinwiddie arrange to put Randolph back in office.

The governor, whether happy or not about the outcome of the fight over the pistole fee, continued to be involved in quarrels over control of the purse. The home government denied his plea that the £20,000 sent him not be reimbursed out of the tobacco export tax. He and his Council were embarrassed and irritated. He was forced to send Virginia money to London. That the money was going across the ocean could not long be concealed from the burgesses, who were the more exasperated because Dinwiddie could spend the royal grant of Virginia money as he wished. After he had left Virginia forever and had submitted to the British Treasury accounts explaining how the money had been disbursed, a committee of the burgesses sought to obtain copies of his vouchers. The accounts were approved by the Treasury, and the committee abandoned its effort to secure the copies. But its request, which could be construed as an expression of suspicion that the governor had engaged in embezzling, angered him.

The burgesses continued to be equally arbitrary with respect to their own appropriations. Dinwiddie wanted to deprive John Robinson of his power over them. Toward that end he considered, in October 1754, a request to the burgesses that they join him in separating the offices of speaker and treasurer. But it was only too obvious that the lower house would refuse. After his final return to Britain Dinwiddie urged that steps be taken to carry through the divorce. His successor, Francis Fauquier, was accordingly ordered, if possible, to secure it. But Fauquier dared not proceed against Robinson; the speaker had far too many friends in Virginia. Besides, said Fauquier, Robinson was a man of "probity."

One reason for Robinson's remarkable popularity was that he did all he could to please his fellow burgesses. He was, perhaps, an honorable man according to his own standards; as is well known, he was afterward remarkably careless about his duties. Given custody of Virginia paper money that had been called in to be destroyed, he instead casually and secretly lent it out to financially embarrassed friends, a cavalier procedure that created a scandal after his death. There is even reason to believe that Robinson lent out public funds for personal profit as early as 1753. Dinwiddie had good grounds for his attempt to reduce Robinson's opportunities to cheat the colony of Virginia.

But Robinson, both liked and trusted in his lifetime, was almost an anti-governor so long as Dinwiddie occupied the Palace in Williamsburg. In order to get more and more money to fight the French, Dinwiddie had to sign bill after revenue bill requiring that expenditures of the proceeds be approved by Robinson's joint committee. With so much control over Virginia money in his hands, the speaker could and did exert power and influence over law making and over the decisions normally within the authority of the executive.

At last, in June 1757, the burgesses decided to let Dinwiddie approve such expenditures, with the advice of the joint committee. That concession to the governor was explained as a measure to relieve the committee of a vast burden of paperwork. It may be that the burgesses had learned to place a measure of trust in the honesty of the governor. In any event, the change came too late to please Dinwiddie greatly, for his period of service in the Palace was drawing to a close.

Chapter 4
War in the West

Virginia's troubles in the time of Dinwiddie extended beyond political squabbles in Williamsburg. The colony's gallows was not entirely unused, nor were the stocks for minor criminals always vacant. A commotion arose at the College of William and Mary in 1757 because professors were intemperate and caused confusion by keeping wives, children, and servants within its intellectual precincts. Tidewater planters worried because the long occupied parts of the colony contained so many Negro slaves and so many convicts exported from Britain to America in supposed effort to improve both countries. More recent settlers in the distant interior of the colony, in the valleys of the Shenandoah and the Kanawha, were wrestling mightily with nature to create farms, homes, churches, and schools. Owning few slaves, they were not concerned about revolt by the blacks, but they had to fear attack by marauding Indians. They suffered enormously from war and rumors of war for a decade after the year 1754.

Virginians who lived on or near the frontiers of the colony —and Marylanders and Pennsylvanians to the northward of them—became concerned for their safety before Dinwiddie took office in Williamsburg. And their anxiety mounted increasingly as the long conflict between Britain and France that had begun in 1689 spread toward them. Hitherto the Virginians had not been immediately menaced by the French or by their Indian allies. Contesting for empire with the British in India, in Africa, in the Caribbean Sea, and in North America, the French claimed for themselves the valley of the St. Lawrence River, the Great Lakes basin, and the valley of the Mississippi River. They were firmly established in their province of Quebec and in their town of New Orleans guarding the mouth of the Mississippi. They also maintained forts at Niagara, Detroit, and Mobile, together with smaller posts in the northern and western parts of the region afterward known as the Old Northwest.

The French did not seek to occupy the lands drained by the Ohio River until after the close of the War of the Austrian Succession—called King George's War in America—in 1748. Then they began aggressively to push southward from Niagara toward the Beautiful River. In so doing, they posed a new challenge, for Britain had never admitted that all of the Mississippi watershed belonged to France, either by the will of the Deity or by discovery. The French advance must provoke a struggle; neither Britain nor her colonists would quietly permit France to check the westward expansion of the Anglo-American settlements at the crest of the Appalachian Mountains. A formal armed clash, and a general resumption of hostilities between France and Britain, therefore became ever more likely.

The Treaty of Aix-la-Chapelle, which brought the War of the Austrian Succession to an official end, proved to be no more than a truce. The fighting ceased only because the several antagonists were weary, not because they had forcibly settled any great issue. Tension quickly mounted between French Quebec and British Nova Scotia. What was more important, the French, having become alarmed because of the presence of British traders in Indian towns north of the Ohio, undertook to drive out those traders and to establish firmly their hegemony over the Miami, Delaware, Shawnee, Huron, Mingo, and other tribes that dwelled in those towns.

British colonials engaged in barter with the redmen had penetrated as far westward as the Wabash River two decades earlier and had been able to undersell French competitors. Mingling politics with business, they had persuaded many Indians that George II rather than Louis XV of France was their great and good friend beyond the distant ocean. Other warriors, shrewder than their fellows, welcomed the traders because they wished to escape complete dependence on the French for the guns, hatchets, clothing, blankets, and liquor that had become necessities for them. In consequence, French influence among those tribes sank during the War of the Austrian Succession. English traders and their Indian clients triumphed in fracases with French rivals and their friends. French officials in Quebec and in Paris feared that British settlers, British soldiers, and the British flag would follow traders from Pennsylvania, Maryland, Virginia, and the Carolinas over the Appalachians.

Hence it was that the marquis de La Galissonière, governor general of New France, sent forth in the summer of 1749 an expedition of regular troops, militia, and Indians. Led by Captain Pierre-Joseph Céloron de Blainville, it aimed to frighten away the British traders and to assert vigorously the authority of France in the Ohio valley. Céloron planted on the banks of the Allegheny and Ohio Rivers lead plates that declared French ownership. He could do little more. Most of the English traffickers in deerskins and beaver defied him, and they were protected by their clients.

Succeeding La Galissonière at Quebec, the marquis de La Jonquière concluded that greater force must be employed to drive away the English civilians, to compel their Indian friends to accept French goods and influence, and to build one or more posts on the Allegheny River or the upper Ohio. La Galissonière championed these proposals in Paris. He successfully urged action to forestall an advance by the English down the Ohio to the Mississippi. That, he pointed out, would sever communications between Canada and Louisiana and would gravely injure the French empire in North America.

In consequence, Chippewa and Ottawa tribesmen led by two Frenchmen took the offensive in June 1752. They attacked and captured a stockade built by the English traders in Pickawillany, a town of the Miami nation on the Great Miami River. They killed several Miami and one trader who tried to defend the fort. The Chippewa and Ottawa warriors ate the chief of the Miami, slain in the fight, and consumed the heart of the trader before they retreated northward with some white-skinned prisoners.

In 1753, despite waning enthusiasm in Paris for bold adventures, the marquis de Duquesne, a new governor general at Quebec, sent out soldiers and workmen who built one fort at Presqu'Isle (now Erie, Pennsylvania) and another, Fort LeBoeuf, on French Creek (now Waterford, Pennsylvania).

Both posts were garrisoned. The English traders were driven back over the Appalachians. The French had nakedly appealed to force in order to assert their right to the valley of the Ohio.

Hindsight may suggest that in throwing down the gauntlet the French were reckless. There were about sixty thousand French settlers in Canada and hardly more than six thousand in Louisiana. Even with the aid of numerous Indian allies, how could they hope to hold back English colonists more than twenty times their number?

Nevertheless, the governors general at Quebec did not issue their challenges in a spirit of desperation. France was much stronger than Britain in population, in wealth, and in armies. Besides, three earlier attempts of the British and their colonists to send expeditions against Quebec had ended in dismal failure. Forests, mountains, and great distances made potent bastions against attacks by land on Canada and Louisiana. Moreover, the English colonists would find it most difficult to mobilize men and resources from fourteen separate governments—they had never been able to exert all their powers or to unite in action. Hence it was that the French on the St. Lawrence dared their Anglo-American enemies to do battle.

Those same circumstances offered no encouragement to the British colonists or to politicians in London. Some colonists even feared that the French would not only come out on top in the Mississippi Valley, but would drive their way eastward to New York Harbor and Chesapeake Bay. The building of two forts at Presqu'Isle and on French Creek therefore caused alarm along the Atlantic seaboard and concern in London. Virginians found no reassurance in news that Indian allies of the French had penetrated the colony's frontiers and had murdered a settler, his wife, and their five children.

It was Robert Dinwiddie who took up the gauntlet. A glance at a modern map would suggest that Pennsylvania should have taken the lead against the aggressors. However, that colony's charter limited it on the west: it was not to extend more than three hundred miles from the Delaware River. Besides, its assembly was dominated by Quakers who were almost as reluctant to vote money for the defense of their commonwealth as they were to bear arms. Maryland, also cramped on the west by its charter, showed somewhat more willingness to act but could muster few men and little money.

Virginia, however, at that time claimed, under its charter of 1609, all territory west of Pennsylvania and Maryland to the Great Lakes and the Mississippi River, as well as the regions afterward formed into the states of West Virginia and Kentucky. The Old Dominion was populous and prosperous. Moreover, Virginian interest in the Ohio Valley was much more than legal, for many leading citizens were members of companies that had secured large grants of land within it from the governor and Council in Williamsburg. One group of speculators had even planted settlers in the watershed of the Kanawha River.

A specially important combination of speculators was the Ohio Company, founded in 1748 by Colonel Thomas Lee. It received permission from London to settle as many as half a million acres near the junction of the Allegheny and Monongahela Rivers—in the area east and south of modern Pittsburgh —and also to engage in trade with the Indians. As early as March 1751 Dinwiddie indicated eagerness to serve its members, and sometime before April 1752 he became a shareholder in it.

That Dinwiddie, as he himself said, had "the success and prosperity of the Ohio Company much at heart," does not force the conclusion that he went forward to meet the French challenge merely in order to defend a personal interest. His investment in its enterprises was probably not large; and it was only one of several in which the governor put his money. His personal interest in the company may well have fortified an almost instinctive desire to oppose national enemies. He wished not only to defend but to expand the American possessions of George II. Later he declared that the British "dominions on this continent" were of a "value not to be estimated" and that "in time, if properly protected," they would form "the western and best empire in the world."

Whatever his motives, Dinwiddie took steps to assert the claims of Britain and of Virginia early in 1752. He sent out commissioners who, in the Treaty of Logstown in June of that year, secured permission from the Indians of the Six Nations for the Ohio Company to build a fort and to found settlements on the southeastern side of the Ohio. In the following autumn he hoped that the Miami tribesmen—he believed that they could put ten thousand warriors in the field—would attack and severely injure the French. The Miami could not muster so many men, and they did not move. He had much to learn about the Indians; and the learning was to be painful.

By December Dinwiddie had concluded that vigorous exertions must be made to check the French. He urged to the Board of Trade the necessity of building two forts and settlements on the Ohio and asked that artillery be sent from England for the defense of the forts. In the following spring he requested the governors of neighboring colonies to help him stop the French—they were invaders of British territories bought from the Indians. Addressing the Board of Trade again on June 16, 1753, he asserted that two French contingents, each containing four hundred men, were reported to be moving southward toward the Ohio; again he pleaded for action.

Dinwiddie's reports of French activity, received in London with similar news from other British governors, stimulated action. British politicians might be commonly indolent, but a threat from detested France could not fail to arouse them. In March 1753 the Board of Trade, under the leadership of its energetic president, the earl of Halifax, informed the earl of Holdernesse, the British cabinet member specially responsible for the welfare and safety of the colonies, that measures must quickly be adopted to stop the "proceedings and encroachments" of France. Were not such steps promptly taken, it was to be feared that the French would entrench themselves and would permanently bar British westward expansion into the interior of North America.

The cabinet, lacking sufficiently reliable information to reach any decision, did not immediately respond to the plea from Halifax. However, the receipt of Dinwiddie's report of June 16 goaded both Halifax and the cabinet. Responding to a second warning from Halifax, the cabinet issued far-reaching orders through Holdernesse on August 28. Its members assumed that the French troops had entered territory that was at least partly British. They authorized Dinwiddie to build his two forts on the Ohio and to employ Virginia militia against the French invaders. They told him not to attack without good reason, but to try to persuade them to withdraw. However, if they "do still endeavour to carry on any such unlawful and unjustifiable proceedings," such as the building of a fort on British territory, "we do hereby strictly charge and command you, to drive them off by force of arms."

All the British governors in North America were similarly commanded to oppose French incursions, and thirty cannon, four-pounders, with eighty barrels of gunpowder, were hastily sent to Virginia. The instructions to Dinwiddie were carried to the Chesapeake in a warship. On second thought, the cabinet decided to give Dinwiddie more help. In January 1754 Holdernesse ordered two independent companies of British regulars stationed at New York and a third one doing garrison duty in South Carolina to proceed to Virginia to assist the governor.

It is apparent that the British cabinet authorized and encouraged Dinwiddie to act. Whether or not hostilities followed, therefore, depended in large part on him. A cautious, timid, or indolent man in his place would doubtless have moved slowly: Had the French actually occupied much, if any, British territory? Was it prudent to risk a clash of arms?

Dinwiddie did not hesitate. In the autumn of 1753, he sent presents to the Indians in the Ohio Valley to win their help or neutrality. And he dispatched "one of the adjutants of the militia here out to the commander of the French forces, to know their intentions, & by what authority they presume to invade His Majesty's dominions in the time of tranquil peace." The adjutant was George Washington, then only twenty-one years old, youthful for such a mission. He made his way to Fort LeBoeuf. To its commander, M. de St. Pierre, he delivered a message from the governor asserting that the French had established themselves within the dominions of Britain and that it had therefore become "my peaceable duty to require your peaceable departure." St. Pierre replied that he would not evacuate his post, that he must refer questions of territorial rights to Quebec. Returning to Williamsburg, Washington informed Dinwiddie that the French were preparing to move further southward in the spring and to build a fort at the junction of the Allegheny and Monongahela rivers, obviously a spot of the greatest strategic importance.

Correctly assuming that the French would indeed resume their military penetration when weather permitted, Dinwiddie energetically prepared to meet their next thrust. To blunt its force he urged the governors of New York and Massachusetts to make a feint toward the St. Lawrence—without result. He begged the governors of Pennsylvania, Maryland, and the Carolinas to raise militia. He called Virginia militia into service. To induce enlistment in a regiment of volunteers to serve on the Ohio, he and his council promised to distribute two hundred thousand acres of land among the men. He tried to persuade Cherokee and Catawba tribesmen as well as Delaware and Miami to take the field. He managed to get an appropriation of £10,000 from the burgesses. But he was not confident that he could thwart the French and regretted that he did not have the help of a regiment of British regulars to assure success.

The British regulars would have been useful. Before spring came, the Ohio Company built one trading post on Redstone Creek and sent men to build another at the forks of the Ohio. Followed by a small detachment of the Virginia regiment, they began in March to erect a fort at the forks. But the French did move forward, and with celerity. Commanding more than one thousand men, Pierre Claude de Contrecoeur floated down the Allegheny River to that strategic spot in April, and demanded and secured the surrender of the thirty-three Virginia troops stationed there.

Dinwiddie had hoped to have five or six companies of the Virginia regiment at Will's Creek in western Maryland by April, together with contingents from Pennsylvania, Maryland, and North Carolina. He lent his own money to the treasury of the Old Dominion in order to put the Virginians in motion. His preparations were incomplete when news reached him that the French had seized the forks of the Ohio and were building their Fort Duquesne there. He resolved, if possible, to drive them away, at least to build a post or posts to check their further advance.

No less determined was young George Washington who,

as lieutenant colonel in the Virginia regiment, commanded an advanced detachment at the Great Meadows. On May 27 he learned that a party of thirty-five or thirty-six Frenchmen led by Ensign Joseph Coulon, sieur de Jumonville, was near his camp. Jumonville had been sent out by Contrecoeur to reconnoitre. If he met British troops west of the Appalachians, he was to tell them to withdraw. If they failed to do so, he was to repel force by force. His instructions were identical in spirit with those given by Dinwiddie to the officers of the Virginia regiment.

It was Washington who actually resorted to gunfire. On May 28, with forty men and some Indian allies, he searched out, surrounded, and attacked Jumonville's force at the Little Meadows. After a short engagement in which ten of the French were slain, including their commander, the remainder surrendered. One Virginian was killed, two or three wounded. Washington's redskin friends scalped some of the dead French soldiers. So began the Seven Years' War in the remote forests beyond the Appalachian divide. It may be contended that both Dinwiddie and Washington were too aggressive, the one in policy, the other in execution. It ought not to be forgotten that the French offered provocation. In any event, once begun, hostilities continued and spread. There followed a long and grinding war.

Whatever may be the moralities of the first clash between the British and French forces, Contrecoeur sought and secured redress. He ordered Captain Louis Coulon de Villiers, brother of Jumonville, to proceed with four hundred soldiers against Washington and to avenge the slayings of Jumonville and his followers. Villiers, accompanied by Indian warriors, appeared on July 3 before a post Washington had established at the Great Meadows and called Fort Necessity. Recently promoted to the colonelcy of the Virginia regiment, Washington had received help, including the company of British regulars from South Carolina. He believed that he could defend Fort Necessity against five hundred Frenchmen.

However, the French and Indians, taking cover behind trees, fired all afternoon at the British forces, who had little protection from their crude fortifications. The French lost few men but the British had thirty killed and seventy wounded by dusk. In consequence, Washington and Captain James Mackay, who commanded the British regulars, agreed to sign articles of capitulation. These referred to the killing of Jumonville as *"l'assassinat,"* and permitted Washington and Mackay to lead the survivors among the garrison back toward the Virginia settlements.

The surrender of Fort Necessity was a severe blow to Dinwiddie. He strove to collect more men to strike at the French. By July one company of British regulars from New York and a body of North Carolina militia had reached Virginia and were available for service. The governor hoped that he could muster enough strength to take Fort Duquesne, even though the French had cannon to defend it. He had learned that he could not rely on Virginia's neighbors to act quickly and decisively. He believed, however, that he could send a force of more than a thousand men against the fort.

He chose as its commander his old and trusted friend, James Innes, a man who had served as a royal soldier and who in 1742 had taken part in the British attack on Cartagena in the War of Jenkins' Ear. He believed that Innes was an able man as well as a veteran. Less confident than he had earlier been, Dinwiddie instructed Innes to assault Fort Duquesne—but if that proved to be unwise, Innes was to build a post beyond the mountains to check further advance by the French.

New difficulties arose. North Carolinians went home before they could render any important service. Dinwiddie had to change his orders: Innes should merely fortify Wills Creek— east of the mountains. The change was the more necessary because Dinwiddie could not then get money for military purposes from the burgesses without sanctioning payment of Peyton Randolph for his activities in the pistole fee dispute— which the governor, of course, declined to do.

By September 6 Dinwiddie was deeply discouraged. He declared a wish to resign. Were he able to do it honorably, he would quit his office, "for I am quite wearied with the many obstacles thrown in my way in discharge of my duty." Rumors of raids by hostile Indians on the frontiers of Virginia worried him. He could then only hope to mount an expedition against the French in the spring of 1755. For the time being, he was compelled to confine his military operations to the protection of the outlying settlements of Virginia.

Dinwiddie received little comfort that autumn from dispatches that came to Williamsburg from London. He learned that Governor Horatio Sharpe of Maryland, a soldier with some experience, had been appointed to command all the British forces sent into the Ohio Valley and that two thousand muskets were coming from England. He was authorized to spend £20,000 from the Virginia treasury to support Sharpe. The burgesses supplied a similar sum. He conferred with Sharpe and Governor Arthur Dobbs of North Carolina at Williamsburg in October.

The three men agreed that the French ought to be driven back, not merely from Fort Duquesne but into Canada. Obviously, it would be most difficult to gather sufficient strength within the colonies to execute such a design. Dinwiddie wrote again and again to London to beg for the help of one or two regiments of regulars, for cannon, for other military equipment. He contended that all the British possessions in North America were endangered by French aggression.

His reports, accompanied by others from various North American governors, deeply disturbed the British cabinet, the more so because France and Britain were quarreling over their respective rights in the Caribbean world and in India as well as in North America. Indeed, most of Dinwiddie's appeals for aid arrived after London decided that they must be heeded. The first reports from the governor concerning the defeat of Washington goaded the government of George II into decisive action. Declared the prime minister, the duke of Newcastle, "All N. America will be lost if these practices are tolerated, and no war can be worse to this country than the suffering such insults as these." Like Dinwiddie, he feared that the French intended to confine the English to the Atlantic seaboard and even ultimately to move eastward to the ocean. "But that is what we must not, we will not, suffer."

Even before Dinwiddie, Dobbs, and Sharpe pessimistically laid their plans for 1755, the duke of Newcastle and his colleagues in the British cabinet took momentous decisions. Under their orders the earl of Albemarle informed the French foreign minister in Paris on September 12 that France must, among other things, withdraw her troops from the region south of Lake Erie if Louis XV sincerely desired to put an end to controversies with Britain. He received an unsatisfactory reply—that France was guilty of neither "invasions or usurpations."

Negotiations continued into the ensuing winter. Newcastle eventually offered a compromise that would have confined the English to the eastern half of the Ohio Valley, but it was rejected in Paris. The French had strengthened their forces overseas after the Treaty of Aix-la-Chapelle, and they were willing to engage quickly in full war to assert their claims.

Britain, too, prepared to fight rather than yield. In that same September the Newcastle ministry called on William Augustus, duke of Cumberland, younger son of George II, a veteran British general, for military advice. He recommended that they send to Virginia the two regiments requested by Dinwiddie and that Major General Edward Braddock be commissioned as commander in chief of the British forces in North America with instructions to drive the French back across Lake Erie. Other British forces should move forward in New York and Nova Scotia to assert British rights. His counsel was accepted. Braddock was instructed even to take the French post at Niagara, if possible.

Both London and Paris knew in the fall of 1754 that British regulars would take the field in North America in the following spring. In February 1755 the government of Louis XV ordered Governor General Duquesne to attack a British post on the Kennebec River; in March it sent three thousand troops across the North Atlantic. Britain responded to those measures with instructions to Admirals Edward Boscawen and Francis Holbourne to attack the fleet that bore the French regulars. Boscawen managed to intercept and capture two French ships and eight companies of troops after a brief struggle off Cape Race. So the war spread to the Atlantic. A year later it was officially declared, and hostilities between Britain and France became general.

There is a temptation to find that the great war resulted from the machinations of the greedy members of the Ohio Company, especially from the activities of one of them, Robert Dinwiddie. Afterward, George Washington declared that such a suspicion existed in Virginia at the beginning of the conflict. Dinwiddie might have said with equal force that Washington precipitated the struggle by attacking Jumonville at the Great Meadows. But the governor made no such accusation. From first to last he put the onus of the war upon the aggressive French—although he never denied that he forthrightly accepted their challenge.

In fact, the war must have come whatever Dinwiddie did. Had the gunfire not begun in the wilderness beyond the Appalachians, it would have commenced on the shores of Lake Ontario, on the border between Quebec and Nova Scotia, in the Caribbean, or in India. For France was determined to wrestle with Britain for empire, and Britain was quite willing to engage. The pleas for help that Dinwiddie sent to London did not compel his superiors to act against their will. They sent the aid he asked for because they sincerely believed that they must counter aggressive encroachments by the French, in the Ohio Valley and elsewhere.

Striving to make ready for another expedition of colonials against Fort Duquesne, Dinwiddie arranged to improve roads toward that place, to collect boats so as to make use of rivers on the route, and to gather supplies. By December 12, 1754 he had received a report that the redcoats would come. He undertook to put at least one thousand Virginia volunteers in the field. Soon after the beginning of the new year he learned that two British regiments were indeed coming to Virginia from garrison forces in Ireland.

At that time he assumed that Governor Sharpe would be placed in command of the regulars. He assured Sharpe that the Virginia troops would be instructed to obey his orders. By January 9 he knew that General Braddock had been appointed to lead both regulars and colonial forces against the French fort. He then hoped that Braddock would reach the Ohio in March, before the French could send reinforcements to Fort Duquesne from Canada—the French would not be able to move until the ice had melted from the lakes and rivers they must traverse. But Braddock could not advance that quickly.

If one cannot find Dinwiddie guilty of precipitating hostilities in order to foster his interest in the Ohio Company, the war nevertheless opened legitimate opportunities to him, and he sought to take advantage of them. Even before the shooting began, despite the fact that he had had no military experience, he began to seek a commission in the British army. Conceiving that it would become necessary for government to choose an officer to command the three independent companies of regulars that were sent to Virginia, he tried to get the appointment for himself. He was so confident that his application would succeed that he ordered a uniform sent from London. The crown might indeed have been wise to place those redcoats under his direction so that they and the Virginia troops would be under the orders of the same person. But his proposal failed to secure approval in London.

In the autumn of 1754 he campaigned, in a series of letters to officials and patrons in the imperial capital, for a truly handsome appointment. As he had foreseen, the officers of the independent regulars and those of the Virginia units quarreled —the British officers would not accept the Virginians as their equals. To remedy that awkward situation he proposed that the Virginia volunteers be taken into royal service and that he himself be given a commission as colonel in the British army. He could cite a precedent for such action, for Governor William Gooch had commanded Virginians in royal pay in the expedition against Cartagena during the War of Jenkins' Ear.

Such an appointment would not have required Dinwiddie to take the field—British colonelcies at that time were often honorary, regiments being led into action by lieutenant colonels. Moreover, a colonelcy was a very valuable piece of property, for its holder received an excellent salary, various perquisites, and retirement on half pay. Alas for the governor, the British decision to send out Braddock destroyed any conceivable need for a Colonel Dinwiddie.

To do the governor justice, it must be said that he desired a successful onslaught on Fort Duquesne far more than he did a colonel's uniform. When Sir John St. Clair, quartermaster general for Braddock, landed in Virginia with positive assurance that the British general and two regiments from Ireland would soon appear in Chesapeake Bay, Dinwiddie gladly undertook to do everything within his power to assist Braddock.

Braddock received a warm welcome when he came to the Palace at Williamsburg, on February 23. Dinwiddie hoped that the coming of the general would "give me some ease, for these 12 months past I have been a perfect slave, and nothing but His Majesty's commands, the national service and the good of these colonies could have prevailed on me to undergo such fatigue." But, said he, he would consider a triumphant expedition led by Braddock as "an agreeable issue to all my troubles." He quickly concluded that Braddock was "a very fine officer" and a sensible, considerate, and honorable gentleman. In fact, he continued to hold a high opinion of that officer, who learned to respect Dinwiddie. When it seemed likely that Braddock would be appointed titular governor to Virginia in succession to the earl of Albemarle, the general indicated that he wished Dinwiddie to continue in office at Williamsburg.

However, not all Virginians subscribed to these sentiments of mutual admiration. One wrote:

> Robin, to common honesty,
> Hath not the least pretence!
> While pride & brutishness supply
> In Ned the place of sense.

Soon after the middle of March all the British troops had reached Virginia, in excellent health despite their long voyage from Cork. Their arrival no doubt raised Dinwiddie's spirits but did not permit him to relax. After their arrival—as before it—he labored constantly in collecting boats, tents, beef, flour, medicines, and all sorts of military paraphernalia to support and assist both Braddock's men and the Virginia troops. His duties frequently fatigued him because Virginia's neighbors gave little assistance, he even had to lend some of his own money again to the public in order to support the Braddock expedition.

In a series of meetings at Alexandria, beginning on March 14 and carried on for a month, Braddock conferred with Dinwiddie and several other British governors. They worked out the details for at least four strokes against the French, and they agreed that the general should have no fewer than three thousand men. Worn out by these deliberations, Dinwiddie remained indoors for several days after his return to Williamsburg to recuperate. His health was suffering from his constant labors, but he continued to do all he could to help Braddock.

The House of Burgesses imposed taxes on lands and on imported Negroes, and also organized a lottery in order to support the general. But problems persisted, and new difficulties developed. Pennsylvania and Maryland failed to supply money to support the general's army; North Carolina gave only a small sum; the bills of exchange for £6,000 that Governor James Glen of South Carolina forwarded reached Braddock after he had begun his march into the wilderness, where he could hardly make use of them. Delay followed delay for Braddock. He encountered a shortage of wagons that was finally remedied by Benjamin Franklin. Dinwiddie tried to secure Cherokee and Catawba warriors to serve as scouts and auxiliaries with Braddock, but Governor Glen persuaded those tribes to confer with him in South Carolina at the very time when they might have been most useful to Braddock.

Nevertheless, Dinwiddie was confident in early June that the general would easily take Fort Duquesne. By that time Braddock's men were crossing the Alleghenies. Dinwiddie was informed that there were no more than six hundred French and hostile redmen at the fort. He felt more concern lest Britain agree to an unfavorable accommodation with France than for the safety of Braddock's forces, and busied himself making arrangements to garrison the French post after its capture. On June 23 Dinwiddie hoped that Braddock's next letter would announce the seizure of the fort, even though the governor had received a report that the French had reinforced its garrison with seven hundred men.

Indeed, Dinwiddie believed that the general would be able both to take Fort Duquesne and to proceed against the French fort at Niagara. He estimated that Braddock would lead three thousand men against twelve hundred French troops and Indian auxiliaries at Fort Duquesne; he hoped that the campaigns of the summer would confine the French "to the barren rocks of Canada." On June 24 he wrote to Captain Robert Orme, who accompanied Braddock, "Pray God protect you all and grant success to our just expedition." News that parties of hostile Indians and Frenchmen had slain Virginia and Maryland frontier settlers distressed him. Sending out militia to prevent further raids, he could comfort himself with the thought that capture of Fort Duquesne would serve to reduce, if not to prevent, such attacks in the future.

Dinwiddie had reason to be confident that Braddock would at least take Fort Duquesne. Washington, who went with the general as a volunteer, also was sure of success. For Braddock led over the Allegheny Mountains no fewer than twenty-two hundred men, of whom about two-thirds were British infantry and artillerymen, the remainder Virginia volunteers. Braddock himself did not doubt that he would carry the fort—he took with him cannon to batter down its defenses. His army moved slowly forward after crossing the mountains.

Informed that five hundred French regulars were on the march southward to strengthen the fort, Braddock tried to hurry his progress by dividing his force. Leaving part of it behind him under Colonel Thomas Dunbar, the general pushed forward with about 1,460 men. Contrecoeur could hardly hope to hold out even against that force. He had available for service only a few companies of French regulars together with some Canadian militia. However, he had been joined by many hundreds of Indian warriors—Braddock, thanks to the interference of Governor Glen, had no such auxiliaries as the day of battle approached.

In desperation, Contrecoeur sent out a mixed body of nine hundred men, more than two-thirds of them Indians, to try to surprise Braddock as he approached the fort. The general knew that ambuscade was a favorite device of the Indians, and he was not shocked when his advanced guard was assailed about mid-day on July 9. But, experienced only in European warfare, he had not thought it necessary to drill his men to fight effectively against enemies firing from forest cover. Attacked in front and then both sides, Braddock's men—most of them in column—could not be persuaded to move against the French and Indians shooting them down from the protection of trees and hills.

The Virginians tried, with some success, to break formation and to fight in Indian style. However, after enduring the fire

Miniature of Robert Dinwiddie by C. Dixon. Possibly painted about 1750 at Bath, when Dinwiddie visited there, it was given to Colonial Williamsburg by Sir Campbell Stuart, a collateral descendant of the governor. (1 ¾ x 1 ⅜ inches)

The Robert Carter House in Williamsburg, which served temporarily as official residence for Governor Dinwiddie and his family. It was built some time before 1746 and was later owned by Robert Carter of Nomini Hall.

The Governor's Palace in Williamsburg, a reconstruction on the original foundations, which remained largely intact when the building burned and collapsed in 1781.

A part of John Mitchell's map of North America, dated 1755. This illustration is reproduced from a copy owned by Colonial Williamsburg.

of their hidden enemies for three hours and suffering heavy losses, the redcoats at last began to break. Braddock was forced to issue the order to retreat, and his shattered army fled in great disorder. Its survivors joined Colonel Dunbar at Little Meadows. Braddock, mortally wounded, died. Dunbar led the remains of the expedition back to Cumberland, Maryland.

Dinwiddie received his first report of Braddock's disastrous defeat and death from Cumberland on July 14. It gave him "much grief and great concern." He hoped that the defeat was "not so bad as reported," that Dunbar had advanced with his detachment to deprive the French of the fruits of their victory.

Until July 24 the governor continued to hope that the first bad news was exaggerated. Then he learned, at Hampton Roads, of enormous losses sustained in the battle on the Monongahela. More than half of Braddock's men were killed, wounded, or captured—some of the captured were afterward tortured and burned at the stake by the Indians at Fort Duquesne. Of eighty-five officers serving under Braddock, sixty-three were slain or injured. Braddock, Sir Peter Halket, colonel of the 44th Regiment, Halket's son, young William Shirley, and other British officers whom Dinwiddie had learned to know and to like, were among the dead. The governor read the sad news "with tears in my eyes."

The Revered Samuel Davies was also grief-stricken. Virginia suffered from drouth that summer; the behavior of her people did not please him; and he was horrified by the slaughter upon and beyond her frontiers. He preached to his congregation at Hanover:

I see thy brazen skies, thy parched soil, thy withering fields, thy hopeless springs, and thy scanty harvests. Methinks I also hear the sound of the trumpet, and see garments rolled in blood—thy frontiers ravaged by revengeful savages; thy territories invaded by French perfidy and violence. Methinks I see slaughtered families, the hairy scalps clotted with gore; the horrid arts of Indian and popish torture. I see the inhabitants generally asleep, and careless of thy fate. I see vice braving the skies; religion neglected and insulted; mirth and folly have still their places of rendezvous.

But Davies was not a pacifist and he did not despair. He issued a poetic call for action to avenge the deaths of Braddock and his brave men:

> A brave revenge alone becomes the brave,
> A brave revenge these dying heroes crave.
> See where their mangled limbs bestrew the field:
> Firm, undismay'd, unknowing how to yield.
> Behold them with their latest gasp of breath,
> Implore their country to revenge their death.

Indeed, more troubles and sorrows lay in store for Virginia.

Chapter 5
Protecting Virginia

S tricken as he was by the defeat and death of Braddock, Dinwiddie neither heaped censure on the unfortunate general for the catastrophe nor accepted the triumph of the French as final. In the midst of his grief he immediately laid plans to renew the offensive against Fort Duquesne.

"I was not brought up to arms," confessed Dinwiddie. But he behaved like a great war minister in the sad days that followed the disaster on the Monongahela. In their panic the retreating redcoats of Britain and bluecoats of Virginia left behind them a train of artillery and large quantities of supplies. Might not the French and their Indians advance along the road built by Braddock and use the abandoned paraphernalia to batter their way into Virginia? Dinwiddie hastily called the militia of the Old Dominion into service to be ready for any eventuality. Then, learning that the enemy, instead of pursuing the beaten British forces, had returned to Fort Duquesne, he strove to inspire a great effort to retrieve the heavy losses of July 9 and to strike again at the French. He called the Virginia assembly into session to help him meet the emergency.

The House of Burgesses was almost as eager as Dinwiddie to make great sacrifices in order to put a reconstructed army in motion. But it proved to be impossible to muster enough power, and Virginia was reduced to the defensive. Securing aid from the Catawba and Cherokee tribesmen, Dinwiddie gained fickle and untrustworthy allies. Frontier families suffered from the onslaughts of the French and hostile Indians; and Colonel George Washington, entrusted with the heavy task of checking their inroads, spent his youthful vigor and health in executing arduous and trying duties. Washington could and did regain his strength. Dinwiddie, nearly forty years older, collapsed from constant strain and never entirely recovered.

Dinwiddie learned from Washington that Colonel Dunbar was considering withdrawal from Fort Cumberland, even thinking of marching to Philadelphia and going into winter quarters. Surely, the governor protested, that officer was not leaving the field in the midst of summer; surely Dunbar did not intend to leave the frontiers of Pennsylvania, Maryland, and Virginia exposed to attack.

Dinwiddie hurriedly sent a messenger to the colonel to urge the necessity of resuming the offensive against the enemy. Let Dunbar rest his men and restore discipline among them. Within a month Dinwiddie would raise at least four or five hundred fresh Virginia troops to enable Dunbar to take the fort—the French at Fort Duquesne would not expect or be prepared for a second struggle. There were cannon enough at Winchester and Fort Cumberland to permit the gathering of a train of artillery to be used against Duquesne. In any event, the French garrison would be surrounded and compelled to surrender.

Assuming that Dunbar would remain for some time at Fort Cumberland, the governor hastened off another courier with a letter to General William Shirley, who had inherited the authority of Braddock as commander in chief. He begged Shirley to order Dunbar to resume the offensive. The least that Dunbar could do, argued Dinwiddie, was to remain at Fort Cumberland so as to offer protection to frontier settlers.

The assembly was receptive to the governor's pleas, Virginia, he declared, was exposed to the "insults of a barbarous and inhuman enemy," whose "base and horrid butcheries" must be checked. Virginia's troops had purchased with their lives "immortal glory to their country and to themselves on the banks of the Monogahela."

The bravery of the Virginians must be matched by military discipline that would enable them to drive away "the brutal savages" and to defend "our helpless wives and poor defenceless babes." He urged the burgesses to supply money handsomely for protection of the colony in general and to offer rewards for the scalps of Indian "beasts of prey" in particular.

The burgesses and the Council acted promptly. They put a price of £10 on Indian and French scalps. The burgesses were willing to supply £60,000, even £100,000, to support twelve hundred Virginia soldiers and a renewed march against Fort Duquesne. They voted only £40,000, however, because more money could not be used.

For the spirited Virginian response to the bad news from the Ohio was unique. Colonel Dunbar ruined Dinwiddie's plan. On August 2 Dunbar marched away from Fort Cumberland with the healthy survivors of the two British regiments and of the three independent companies that had served under Braddock. He moved toward Philadelphia—to go into winter quarters there—leaving behind him at Fort Cumberland and Winchester only Virginia troops, a few Marylanders, and sick and wounded men of the 44th and 48th Regiments. Virginia could not of herself muster, equip, and train enough men in time to strike at Duquesne before winter came. Accordingly, the burgesses provided money only for defensive purposes.

The departure of Dunbar for the safety and comforts of Philadelphia infuriated Dinwiddie—and Dunbar's decision could not be reversed. Dinwiddie's plea to General Shirley for a second march against Duquesne induced the new commander in chief to instruct Dunbar to resume the offensive, if possible. His orders did not reach Dunbar, however, until the defeated redcoats were well on their way to the Pennsylvania capital. It was then too late for Dunbar to retrace his steps— at least that officer so concluded after a council of war.

Immediately after Braddock's defeat Dinwiddie rather expected that he would be replaced by a military man, better equipped than he to meet an emergency. Tired and bitterly disappointed, he praised the Virginians for the valor they had displayed on that dismal July 9. But what had Braddock and his regulars accomplished? They had built a road that made it easier for the French and their savage allies to invade Virginia. And Dunbar had marched away in the middle of summer toward winter quarters.

Dinwiddie was accused in Virginia of favoring Scots. But he had dealt forcefully with Scottish Surveyor General Dunbar; he now castigated Scottish Colonel Dunbar. He wrote

to Captain Robert Orme that "your great Colonel has gone
to a peaceable colony," that "nothing could divert" Dunbar
"from his determin'd retreat." Dinwiddie almost as forthrightly denounced that officer in reports to the British
ministry.

Condemning the behavior of Dunbar as "monstrous" in letters to Governor Horatio Sharpe of Maryland and Governor
James DeLancey of New York, and as "pusillanimous" in one
to William Allen of Philadelphia, Dinwiddie pointed out that
Dunbar had even taken with him the remnants of the three
companies of independent regulars specifically sent to protect
Virginia. Besides, discouraged by the departure of the redcoats for serene scenes in eastern Pennsylvania, the Virginia
troops who survived the slaughter on the Monongahela began
to desert in dozens.

Nevertheless, the governor declined to admit that the British
must assume a defensive posture during the remainder of the
year 1755. By late August he had put in motion six companies
of rangers to cover the frontier settlements of Virginia and
was arranging to build blockhouses for the same purpose. But
he was not content. Undertaking to raise and supply twelve
hundred men for another march over the Alleghenies, he
begged the governors of Maryland and Pennsylvania to fur-
nish men to assist the Virginians. Dinwiddie proposed that
the troops from the three colonies build a post on the western
side of the mountains as a counterbalance to Fort Duquesne
and that they undertake to maintain a garrison of eight hundred men in it. Cannon to defend it were available. Success
in that enterprise would not only restore morale among the
colonists but would facilitate an attack upon Duquesne in
1756.

But Dinwiddie learned quickly that his scheme could not
be executed: Pennsylvania would raise no troops. At the end
of August he considered a proposal from Virginia Colonel
William Fitzhugh, who indicated that he was willing to lead
four or five thousand horsemen against Duquesne. Unencum-
bered by a train of artillery, those mounted troops could move
rapidly against the French post. Dinwiddie was compelled to
reply that such "a bold attempt," such "a desperate attack,"
entailed great risks. How could the horsemen take a fort de-

fended by cannon? Besides, it was impossible to find quickly
so many men and horses. Dinwiddie had no choice but to
abandon hope of resuming the offensive in 1755.

The governor assumed a defensive posture most reluctantly.
Raids by hostile redmen could be finally and decisively
checked, as Dinwiddie well knew, only by driving away their
European friends. Forced to leave the French in possession
of the forks of the Ohio, unable even to erect a post beyond
the Alleghenies as a counterbalance to Duquesne, the governor soon learned that parties of Shawnee and other enemy
Indians were indeed ravaging the outlying settlements of
Virginia.

The savages swarmed past a garrison holding Fort Cumberland and also penetrated far into the Shenandoah valley. They
even appeared near Fort Loudoun at Winchester, the principal
post in the Shenandoah. The Indians burned cabins, destroyed
crops, and killed more than seventy frontier folk. From Fort
Cumberland Colonel Adam Stephen reported that they "spare
the lives of the young women, and carry them away to gratify
the brutal passions of lawless savages," and that the smoke of
burning plantations darkened the day and hid the neighboring
mountains. The Reverend Samuel Davies reported that

Our frontiers have streamed with British blood. There you might
see flourishing plantations deserted; families scattered or butch-
ered; some mangled and scalped; some escaped in horror and con-
sternation, with the loss of their earthly all; some captivated by
the savages, dragged through woods and swamps, and mountains
to their towns, and then prostituted to barbarous lust, or condemned to lingering tortures, which, I believe, have hardly ever
been equalled on this side hell.

The backwoodsmen panicked. Many of them fled eastward
to seek safety. The rangers raised by Dinwiddie could not
catch the rapidly moving redmen. With the support of the
House of Burgesses he undertook to enlist and maintain an en-
larged regiment of one thousand volunteers that could stop
any major attack. In command of that regiment he placed
young George Washington, who had displayed great gallantry in the battle of the Monongahela. He hoped that Washington would be able not only to recruit the regiment, but to

drill it and to develop in his men some efficiency in "bush fighting," so that they could act aggressively in 1756. For the moment all of the measures undertaken by Dinwiddie were palliatives. Washington found it difficult to secure volunteers. The raids of the enemy Indians ceased only with the coming of winter.

Was there no way to strike back at Virginia's enemies? Dinwiddie found one. If he could not assault Fort Duquesne, he could hit at the marauding Shawnee. Cannon were not needed to attack their villages beyond the Ohio. The governor sent out 230 mounted men under Major Andrew Lewis, together with a contingent of 80 Cherokee warriors, to surprise the Shawnee in mid-winter. But snow, rain, and floods impeded Lewis's progress. He and his men finally had to kill their horses for food, and to return without firing a shot at a Shawnee. They captured three harmless French civilians.

The failure of the expedition against the Shawnee did not discourage Dinwiddie from seeking the help of the Cherokee, who could send as many as twenty-five hundred warriors into battle. He had entertained a delegation from that nation at Williamsburg in 1752; he had conferred with Cherokee leaders at Winchester in 1754; and he had sent presents to their towns to gain their friendship. It was a severe disappointment to him that Governor James Glen of South Carolina had convened a great gathering of Cherokee in June 1755, in order to buy land from them, at the very time when Braddock was marching to his death. Glen had not only failed to try to induce those Indians to join Braddock, he had persuaded them to sell an excessive amount of land—a sale that would later turn them against the encroaching British.

Dinwiddie knew that Glen could have sent northward Cherokee warriors who might well have saved Braddock from crushing defeat. He condemned Glen's conduct—and rightly —in language almost as vigorous as he used in castigating Dunbar. He did not hesitate to tell Glen and the British ministry that the South Carolina governor, another Scot, had grossly neglected his duty.

Learning that Glen had been replaced, Dinwiddie eagerly sought the help of the Cherokee, and also of the less numerous Catawba, for the campaign of 1756. With the support of the

Virginia Assembly he sent out William Byrd III and Peter Randolph, members of his Council, with handsome presents to confer with leaders of the two nations. The Cherokee promised to supply six hundred fighting men if Virginia would build a fort to help them defend their country against incursions by the French and their allies. Dinwiddie then commissioned Major Andrew Lewis with sixty men to erect the post. Almost simultaneously South Carolinians established and garrisoned a second fort among the Cherokee. Those Indians were therefore as thoroughly committed as they could be to supply auxiliaries for service on and beyond the frontiers of Virginia. The Catawba also gave pledges to Byrd and Randolph that they would take up the hatchet.

Useful as Cherokee and Catawba warriors might be, Dinwiddie could not be confident that he had turned the balance of strength in favor of the British. Other British commanders in North America had fared better than Braddock in the campaigns of 1755. The French had been checked on the borders of Nova Scotia, and General William Johnson had defeated a French army under the Baron Dieskau in the battle of Lake George. But General Shirley had failed to move westward against Niagara.

On the day before Christmas in 1755 the governor once again signed an appeal to London for military help. Good British officers and good British troops would be needed in America for the campaign of 1756. William Shirley, in part because he was not a professional soldier, in part because he was feuding with Sir William Johnson, who could enlist the aid of the Iroquois nations, ought not to continue as commander in chief. Dinwiddie sensibly urged that he be replaced by a British general and that another officer be sent from England to lead an expedition to the Ohio. Dinwiddie also warned against reliance on the Virginia militia, for "our people want a martial spirit." Besides, he could not get authority from the burgesses to send the militia beyond the boundaries of the Old Dominion.

His disparagement of the Virginians as less than brave is somewhat surprising in view of the fact that they performed better than the redcoats in the battle of the Monongahela. But such was his considered opinion, one that he often expressed.

The redcoats fell into panic once; the Virginians behaved badly on many occasions. He commonly applied the adjectives "cowardly" and "dastardly" to undisciplined Virginia militia.

Dinwiddie did not receive more redcoat help, either from Britain or from the contingents serving under William Shirley. Indeed, Shirley, laying plans for advances toward Montreal and Niagara, asked Virginia to send 1,750 men northward to assist him and also to play a principal role in another march against Fort Niagara. To be sure, the capture of Montreal or of Niagara would cut off the supply lines of the French to Fort Duquesne and to their Indian allies south of the Great Lakes and would eventually reduce both the garrison of that fort and its redskin auxiliaries to impotence.

But the burgesses were concerned for the immediate safety of Virginia, and refused to supply troops for service in New York or Canada. Besides, so many men could not be enlisted or drafted for service in a distant theatre of war. The burgesses would not even vote money for the support of troops serving in New York. Accordingly, Dinwiddie proposed instead to Shirley, and to the earl of Loudoun, who came from England to succeed Shirley, that a British officer lead militia of Pennsylvania, Maryland, Virginia, and North Carolina, together with Cherokee auxiliaries, against Fort Duquesne. British engineers would also be needed for that venture. Shirley commissioned Governor Sharpe as commander of the proposed expedition, but would do no more. Nor did Loudoun offer any substantial assistance.

It would be absurd to criticize Shirley or Loudoun, even though neither of those men was a military genius, for neglecting Virginia—unless one condemns the appointment of Sharpe, as did the anonymous critic of Dinwiddie so often quoted in these pages. He asked satirically why Shirley did not appoint "some staid elderly *Mon*, that has been bred up on the way of turning the penny the rite way, into his own pocket." The two generals had to face the bulk of French power concentrated on the St. Lawrence. Surely the Virginians and their colonial neighbors could deal with the French contingents on the Allegheny and at the forks of the Ohio, even though those small bodies of troops were supported by Indians.

Had the Pennsylvanians, Marylanders, Virginians, and North Carolinians mustered their very real power, they could have assailed Fort Duquesne with overwhelming forces. Indeed, Virginia alone possessed ample men and money to drive the French and their Indian allies beyond Lake Erie. But the colonists would not, could not, mobilize for a great offensive effort. It did not seem worthwhile to the majority of Virginians—or their neighbors—to make the necessary sacrifices.

Instead, not a few Virginians cared only about defending their own colony, while citizens of Pennsylvania, Maryland, and North Carolina showed even less concern about the progress of the war. During many months after the beginning of the conflict the legislatures of Maryland and Pennsylvania refused to supply cash for military purposes unless the proprietors, the Calvert and Penn families, permitted taxation of lands that remained in their hands. And governors defending the property rights of the proprietors refused to raise money on such terms. The Pennsylvania Quakers, opposed to warfare on principle, balked at voting defense funds, with or without cloying conditions. The record of the House of Burgesses was far better, with respect to carrying on the war, than those of its counterparts in Annapolis and Philadelphia. But the burgesses made less than immense sacrifices, in part because they did not properly assess the power of the Old Dominion.

The appearance of more than one thousand exiled French Acadians in Hampton Roads in November 1755 aroused alarm as well as anger in Williamsburg. Dinwiddie persuaded his Council, with difficulty, to make provision for them during the winter. He sought to find lands on which they could settle, although he feared that they might prove to be troublesome enemies, perhaps encouraging slave revolts within Virginia and French and Indian attacks from without. The burgesses would not permit the exiles to remain in the colony. In the spring of 1756 they supplied money to send those "intestine enemies" away from Virginia allowing the French families to go where they willed, even back to Nova Scotia. However, Dinwiddie persuaded the burgesses to put the exiles aboard ship for England, so that they could be transported to France. When fifty more Acadians, expelled from South Carolina, entered Chesapeake Bay, Dinwiddie ordered the master of the ship which carried them to take them back to that colony. He had done what he could to provide for the exiles.

The treatment accorded to the Acadian expatriates by Virginia was not liberal. The Council and the House of Burgesses were neither willing to let them settle in the Old Dominion nor eager to provide food and shelter for them until they could be sent elsewhere. Virginians were overswayed by their fear and detestation of France. But they had reason to dread and hate the French nation. Even as the Acadians sailed away, hostile Indians, sent out from Fort Duquesne and led by Frenchmen, began a new series of raids on the frontiers of Virginia.

The spring of 1756 was a sad time for the backwoodsmen of the Old Dominion. Moving with their customary rapidity and stealth, the redmen avoided strong places like Fort Cumberland and Fort Loudoun, where they must face bodies of militia. They raided farms and captured small blockhouses. Colonel George Washington reported from Fort Loudoun that their bloody incursions could hardly be checked. He feared that "the Indians and their *more* cruel associates" might compel the backwoodsmen and their families to retreat eastward across the Blue Ridge. Washington concluded that it would be necessary to draft men for service on the frontier in order to check the red and white savages. Dinwiddie called out the militia of ten western Virginia counties to help in the emergency. So great was the panic in Williamsburg that scores of gentlemen volunteered to go to the scene of action. Before they could act, the marauders, having done as much damage as they might, retreated into the forests from which they came.

The punishing raids of the Indians and French stirred the burgesses to action. Accepting the advice of Washington and Dinwiddie, they authorized the drafting of enough men to raise the number of troops in the service of the Old Dominion to fifteen hundred; they also voted £25,000 to support the Virginia soldiers and £35,000 toward the expense of another expedition against Fort Duquesne. Even so, without help from British forces, the governor despaired of achieving more than an unsatisfactory defense of his colony. In that spring of 1756 Pennsylvania finally raised £60,000 for military purposes, but only to contain attacks by French and Indian enemies. And Maryland at length undertook to raise troops, but only two hundred men. Besides, cannon needed to attack Fort Duquesne successfully had been taken from Virginia for use elsewhere. It would serve no purpose to move against the fort without such guns and without engineers. Dinwiddie sent Councilor Philip Ludwell to New York City to make a personal plea to Lord Loudoun for help.

By that time Dinwiddie was suffering from both "fatigue of body and vexation of mind." As early as February 1756 he wrote to his good friend, James Abercromby, who had been appointed agent in London for the governor and the Council, at the insistence of Dinwiddie: "I am quite wore out, and the complaint that occasioned my going to the Bath some time before I left England is returned on me so that a new governor would give me no disgust; though, while we are in a state of war here, I would not apply for leave to come home, unless my complaint increases."

What was the affliction that had sent him to Bath before he took office as governor and that now returned? Probably he suffered from gout or arthritis, for it was commonly believed that the mineral waters of Bath alleviated those ailments. His condition worsened. In June he said in another letter to Abercromby, "I am really in a bad state of health." He declared that unless he recovered during the summer, "I must in the fall desire leave to come home, as I am convinc'd the Bath would be of much service to me."

His health did not improve. In July he expressed hope that he would be allowed to return to Britain in the spring of 1757. In September he wrote to Lord Halifax that he had been seized by "a paralytic disorder that gives me great uneasiness," to Abercromby that the onset of the paralysis was recent, that it "reaches my head, and gives me a great deal of concern." He then expressed belief that his condition required relief from his duties and leave to go to England.

On October 28 he formally solicited permission from Lord Loudoun to leave his post—the "paralytick disorder in my head" rendered him "incapable of discharging the requisites of my appointment in so regular and exact a maner as I could wish." He had then been confined to the Governor's Palace for a fortnight. "I dread the consequence of my complaint," he wrote to Sir John St. Clair on October 29. It was accompanied by fever. He reported to Abercromby in a letter of November 9 that "I have been greatly indispos'd and confin'd to my room, and it's pain for me to write." On January 4, 1757 he was "still in a badd state of health, and greatly reduc'd."

The governor had reached the seventh decade of his life, and failing health could have been no surprise in any case. But Dinwiddie for most of his years in Virginia had labored under a burden of cares that might have staggered a younger man. His ample official correspondence reveals beyond cavil that he never shirked his duties, and they were many. He had to cajole and conjure the burgesses and the Council. He was obliged to make a host of appointments, civil as well as military. Ought there not be a British warship off the Chesapeake to protect Virginia commerce? He begged for one until the Admiralty heeded his pleas. Should he put his name on death warrants for Washington's men convicted of desertion? He signed some. What ought to be done about the College of William and Mary, increasingly plagued by dissension? He finally reported the situation to the bishop of London. Should he permit the issuance of paper money by Virginia, despite the fact that his superiors in London frowned on such emissions? He did, in 1756, for currency was very scarce in the colony. Ought not Maryland join Virginia in the erection of a lighthouse at the mouth of Chesapeake Bay? He asked for, but did not secure, the help of Maryland. He had to entertain many visitors to Williamsburg. His private business must have been extensive.

And always there was the war, the raising and supplying of troops, exasperating negotiations with friendly but fickle Indians, the making of military plans that could not be executed, raids by hostile redmen, and that garrison of Frenchmen at Fort Duquesne that could not be dislodged.

To all these troubles must be added personal abuse heaped upon him by various enemies in and out of the House of Burgesses. One of his detractors, Francis Farguson, a resident of the Shenandoah valley, perhaps a man maddened by Indian raids, was arrested by the sheriff of Augusta County for "damning" Dinwiddie as a "Scotch pedling son of a bitch." Farguson was found guilty in court of misconduct, but went free after apologizing and giving security to keep the peace. Another nasty critic, a Mr. Hedgeman, sorely vexed Dinwiddie by attacking him "in a villainous manner and with great injustice." The governor undertook to bring Hedgeman into court at Williamsburg to sue him for slander or libel in order to make an example of him.

Dinwiddie continued throughout 1756 to plead for an expedition against Fort Duquesne. An attack on it was "much more eligible than sauntering on our frontiers on the defensive." Were that post not taken, "we shall be forever exposed" to invasions, murders, and robberies, he informed Lord Loudoun. If an attack failed, at least the French would be forced to divert part of their strength to hold the post.

But it was useless to appeal to the general for help. Arriving at New York City late in July, that officer faced many troubles. Shirley had accomplished nothing. Moreover, the marquis de Montcalm had come to Canada. Soon after the appearance of Loudoun in America, Montcalm captured the British post at Oswego; and Loudoun could find no way to retrieve that small disaster. Instead of supplying assistance to Virginia, he begged Dinwiddie to enlist Virginians in British royal American regiments for service in the north. Regretfully but loyally, the governor urged men to join the general's forces and collected two hundred recruits. Loudoun also asked that Virginia supply money for the expenses of his army. To this the burgesses would not comply—Virginia money was needed for the defense of Virginia.

In the fall of 1756 Dinwiddie even worried a bit lest Fort Cumberland fall to the French. But he expected to hold it, and he hoped—almost against hope—that a move against Fort Duquesne in the following spring would at last become feasible. Meanwhile, could not Major Andrew Lewis try again to strike at the Shawnee with Virginians and Cherokee? Impossible; Cherokee warriors did not appear. When Washington collected more than enough troops to garrison Fort Cumberland, he could also strengthen Fort Loudoun at Winchester and smaller posts, thus assuring the Virginia backwoodsmen somewhat better protection.

Washington, like Dinwiddie, could hardly have done more than he did; but critics savagely condemned him for supposed inactivity. This despite the fact that more than one hundred of Washington's men were killed or wounded in the campaign of 1756. Near the end of October, Dinwiddie reported to London, with pain, "We have every week fresh alarms from our frontiers of the barbarous murders committed on our poor settlers." He emphasized that all the "sculking parties" of French and Indian raiders could not be stopped.

The new year brought more disappointments and troubles to Dinwiddie. Militia officers on the Virginia frontier planned a raid against the Shawnee, but could not collect enough men to undertake it. Though tired and sick, the governor went to Philadelphia in the midst of winter to attend a conference called by Lord Loudoun to concert measures for the coming campaign. There he waited with other governors for three weeks until the general appeared from New York City. "I'm very weary of the place, and want to return home," he wrote to his friend John Blair, senior member of the Council in Williamsburg.

Loudoun's arrival gave Dinwiddie no grounds to believe that the general would act to remove the French and Indian menace from the borders of Virginia. Burdened with the heavy task of taking the French strongholds in Canada—an assignment that he utterly failed to execute—Loudoun neither would nor could help to mount an offensive toward the Ohio. Indeed, Dinwiddie, convinced that the French would attack South Carolina, promised Loudoun that he would try to send four hundred Virginians to help defend that colony. He could send only two hundred, as it turned out, and they were not needed—French warships did not appear off Charleston bar, French soldiers did not land at Beaufort. Meanwhile, alarms came, as they had ever since Braddock's defeat, from western Virginia.

Frustrated, exhausted, and ill, Dinwiddie submitted his resignation as governor from Philadelphia. He conferred with Loudoun, who gave his consent to Dinwiddie's departure for England, and the two men agreed to recommend as his successor Colonel John Young, a friend of the general. Accordingly, Dinwiddie wrote to William Pitt, who had assumed direction of the British war effort in London, to ask for "leave of absence" and permission to leave Virginia—in effect, to sail for England and to continue to draw his pay until Colonel Young or some other person should be appointed in his stead. He requested his friends James Abercromby and Lord Halifax to arrange as soon as possible for his relief from office in Williamsburg. Could Abercromby arrange for passage of the Dinwiddie family across the Atlantic on a British warship?

After his return to Williamsburg at the end of March the governor suffered from "a violent cold." His condition in general continued for some time to be dubious, virtually confining him to his room for six weeks. He announced his intention to retire to the Council and the House of Burgesses in mid-April, and in May he wrote Abercromby that he must be relieved as "an absolute necessity." But from London he received no reply to his request for many long months, although he urged again and again that it be approved.

In June he felt well enough to inform his friend, Governor Arthur Dobbs of North Carolina, that "I've not yet recover'd my health, tho' somewhat better." The improvement in his condition was fortunate, for he could not leave Virginia until the year 1757 had ended. Delay followed delay in London: the British cabinet was unsettled; officers of state enjoyed their customary summer holidays; and an attack of the gout kept Lord Halifax from attending to business for a time.

Furthermore, a successor could not quickly be chosen—the candidacy of John Young having been set aside because he sought to be simultaneously both a lieutenant colonel and a lieutenant governor. Obviously Young could not serve in both capacities, although he was so confident of becoming lieutenant governor, it is related, that he sent a post-chaise to Virginia so he could ride in suitable state.

The Board of Trade considered on June 23 a memorial from Dinwiddie in which he declared that he was "in a very dangerous state of health," and that he had "no hopes left for his recovery while he continues in America." The very next day the earl of Holdernesse wrote a letter authorizing Dinwiddie to return to England on leave. But the letter was apparently retained in London for some weeks. In August Dinwiddie was "so much indispos'd" that he could not write a letter. "Fever and ague" confined him to his house for almost three weeks. At last, late in September, he received permission to return to England even though his successor had not been chosen. He made arrangements to sail in November, but was forced to remain in Virginia, because of lack of suitable transportation until January of the following year.

Dinwiddie at last had to abandon hope of devising some military scheme that would raise the British flag over Fort Duquesne. For the campaign of 1757 Lord Loudoun stationed Brigadier General John Stanwix at Carlisle, Pennsylvania, with a small body of British troops to ward off French and Indian incursions. Maryland supplied 150 men to garrison Fort Cumberland. Indian allies came northward to help the Virginians. Dinwiddie learned in the summer of that year that the garrison of Fort Duquesne numbered only 150 men. Was it not possible to take the offensive? It was not. Other officials lacked his ardor. As usual, the several colonies that would have profited from reduction of the French post could not concentrate their strength to achieve it.

On the other hand, their common enemies were active. In June a body of French and Indians marched southward from Fort Duquesne. Their movement created panic. Reports reaching Dinwiddie caused him to fear that Fort Cumberland would be lost. It turned out that the French and Indians had no cannon and that Fort Cumberland was safe. They were merely raiders. But they were preceded and followed by other raiders, and the Virginia frontiersmen once more felt the brutal force of tomahawk and torch. However, the blows aimed at them were somewhat blunted, for Indians who were friends of King George were taking the field and harassing his white and red enemies.

In the spring of 1757 Dinwiddie's efforts to get Indian help at last began to bear important fruit. In April and May about four hundred warriors, chiefly Cherokee and Catawba, but including Tuscarora, moved northward into the Shenandoah valley to take part in the war. A few of the redmen still resident in Virginia, Nottaway and Saponey, also took up the hatchet. Dinwiddie instructed Washington to send out parties of those allies "a scalping," and "to observe the motions of the enemy." Thereafter, bands of friendly warriors inflicted both casualties and cruelties on the French and their Indian auxiliaries. Washington reported that some Cherokee led by Lieutenant Baker attacked ten Frenchmen near Fort Duquesne, captured one, and killed and scalped five. Thus the French and their forest allies were compelled to reduce their onslaughts on the frontiers of the British colonies.

The burgesses, as eager as Dinwiddie to secure Indian auxiliaries, showed greater disposition than ever to spend money in order to carry on the war. They voted £80,000 to maintain fifteen hundred men in military service, and they imposed land and poll taxes to raise that sum. Besides, they furnished £3,000 for presents to Indian friends and another £5,000 to purchase goods to be sold to them at cost in order to assure their good will. Dinwiddie was then able to boast to William Pitt that Virginia had contributed its full share to the war effort, even though the resulting achievements were meager.

Resort to enlistment of Indian auxiliaries was a hazardous expedient, as Dinwiddie had long since learned. Proximity of red and white men bred contempt and even hatred. Indians came and went to and from Winchester and Williamsburg. They quarreled among themselves and with white settlers and officers. They bedeviled Washington at Fort Loudoun with complaints and demands for presents.

Both Washington and Dinwiddie sighed with relief when Edmund Atkin, a South Carolinian who had received a royal appointment as superintendent of Indian affairs for the tribes beyond the frontiers of the southern colonies, appeared in Virginia from New York. They hoped that Atkin would be able to calm dissatisfied and restless Cherokee warriors. But Atkin was of little use. After some weeks at Winchester he went on to Charleston, leaving behind him Cherokee more disgruntled than they were before his appearance. Eventually, indeed, the friendship between the English and the Cherokee nation would be overstrained. The little and indecisive help given by those Indians in 1757 and later was dearly bought, and in 1760 the Cherokee took the warpath against the English colonists.

There can be no doubt that Dinwiddie gladly left America for the last time, and not merely because his health had failed. Try as he might, he was condemned by captious and suspicious Virginians. In his last year of office the burgesses begged that he cancel an embargo placed on export shipping at the behest of Lord Loudoun so that the general could get transports and take an army to Cape Breton Island without arousing the attention of the French. Ships loaded with tobacco and grain were rocking idly and expensively in Virginia harbors and at the docks of the planters. After considering the request with the Council, Dinwiddie at length judged it necessary to permit the ships to sail. Thereupon Governor Horatio Sharpe of Maryland permitted vessels kept in the harbors of his colony to go to sea. New England governors independently took the same action about the same time.

Whether the embargo was militarily useful is doubtful, but Lord Loudoun was furious. The general conceived that he might be charged, in connivance with Dinwiddie, of favoring Virginia. Loudoun also concluded that Dinwiddie had a pecuniary interest in the Virginia vessels and that the governor acted to protect it. He reported his belief to the duke of Cumberland and to Lord Halifax and suggested that Dinwiddie be recalled rather than permitted to resign. Later, in September, Loudoun indicated to Dinwiddie that he no longer harbored the suspicion.

It is most unlikely that the wealthy governor would so obviously have risked censure in order to save or make a few hundred pounds. In fact, no good evidence has been found that he had a pecuniary stake in either a ship or a cargo. But William Byrd III reported to Loudoun in November that he had received a letter from Virginia which declared that the Virginia Council had acted at the urging of Dinwiddie; that several of its members opposed the lifting of the embargo; that the governor allowed ships to leave Virginia harbors even before the embargo was removed; that "it was believed he was deeply concerned in the cargoes"; that Dinwiddie had violated earlier embargoes; and that his operations, being executed through his friend John Hunter, contracting agent for the army and navy in Virginia, and "his clark" Mr. Rolston, were well concealed.

If the accusation was valid, Dinwiddie did indeed hide his guilt—if there was guilt in refusing to execute the embargo. Anyone who reads the extensive correspondence of the governor, however, will doubt that he was unscrupulous about money. In all probability he was the victim of an unwarranted attack by an enemy without a name.

The House of Burgesses officially expressed regret that Dinwiddie was departing; the Council and the corporation of Williamsburg declared their sorrow, surely with greater sincerity; and it is likely that the common council of Norfolk was not merely polite when it thanked him for kind services and expressed its wish that his voyage be agreeable and that he enjoy "a happy recess from the trials and fatigues of government." The Reverend Thomas Dawson, John Blair, and Colonel Richard Corbin, all of them members of his Council, were quite sincerely affected. Dawson had lost a powerful friend. He had found the Dinwiddies, husband and wife, "courteous and affable," "easy and agreeable to all their acquaintances." Blair, assuming temporarily the powers of governor, officially referred to Dinwiddie as a "worthy" man. It will be recalled that the Reverend Samuel Davies had also developed a liking for Dinwiddie.

In the autumn of 1757 the Dinwiddies busily prepared to depart. The governor commissioned Colonel Corbin to sell his slaves and his furniture, and to collect many debts owed him by various Virginians. His attempt to secure passage on a British warship failed. Although a French privateer might attack an unarmed merchant ship, he decided not to wait until he could embark on a warship. The day before Christmas he expected to sail within eight or ten days. He made arrangements to go aboard the *Baltimore* of Captain Cruikshanks. There was further delay. At last, on January 11, he said farewell to the Council. The *Baltimore* went to sea on the following day.

Dinwiddie did not leave Virginia in official disfavor. He was not recalled because of General Loudoun's attack on him— Lord Halifax knew Dinwiddie too well to be much affected by the accusation. Besides, there was nothing to be gained by insulting Dinwiddie.

But it is only too apparent that the governor did not go

home in a blaze of glory. Despite all his efforts, the French were still entrenched in Fort Duquesne, and Virginia still suffered from incursions by hostile Indians. He could be praised only as a man who had done his best amid the most trying circumstances. He could console himself with the thought that he was in no way responsible for the military disasters that befell Braddock, Shirley, and Loudoun. Loudoun himself proved to be a miserable failure and was recalled in disgrace—the punishment he had proposed for Dinwiddie.

Chapter 6
British Imperialist

N o monument to Robert Dinwiddie towers over London's
Trafalgar Square like that of Lord Nelson, no memorial
to him jostles the small statue there of George Washington. It
was his fate that other servants of the British empire should far
surpass him in achievement. But no one in the overseas employ
of Britain excelled him in devotion to duty or in loyalty to his
country. He continued throughout life to give his political affection to the government of the British Isles. Accordingly, he
struggled to defend and expand the empire at the expense of
France, and tried almost as hard to expand the authority of the
home government over Britain's colonies on the North American mainland. He was not, he did not become in any way, an
American.

How could it have been otherwise? The allegiances of childhood might indeed have been overcome. Had he settled in
youth on a Virginia plantation, had he married a Virginian, he
might have acquired American economic interests and familial
ties, and with them local notions about the right relationship
between colonists and their mother country. His residence in
Bermuda did not decisively turn him away from the land of his
birth. Becoming a British official, he assumed duties that required him to defend imperial power and to protect and enhance British maritime commerce, even at the expense of
colonial prosperity. His permanent appointment as surveyor
general attached him financially to Britain. Returning to Virginia as governor late in the sixth decade of life, he was doubtless too old to change. Besides, he was pledged as governor to
protect the rights of the crown against colonial encroachments
and to guard the economic welfare of Britain against attack by
Virginians solicitous for their own prosperity.

As a royal governor Dinwiddie could hardly have avoided struggles with the Virginians except by violating his trust. John Robinson, Peyton Randolph, Landon Carter, and other Virginians who fought against him were not meek and mild men. They eagerly asserted themselves and their rights. What his conscience permitted him to do to please the Virginians, he did; but there were limits beyond which he could not and would not go to satisfy them. On occasion he stood as stubbornly as they; and he did not always control his temper. Bold enough to condemn officially the behavior of Governor Glen and Colonel Dunbar, to incur their enmity, and to risk reproof from London in consequence, he did not shrink from using strong language about—and to—colonials who aroused his anger.

It has been observed that the animosities stimulated by the quarrels over the presidency of William and Mary and over the pistole fee survived settlement of those issues. In the summer of 1757 Dinwiddie berated Peyton Randolph, apparently with good reason, because Randolph as attorney general casually permitted a violator of the British Navigation Acts to escape punishment. The trials of the early years of the Seven Years' War, including Braddock's defeat and the chronic raids of the French and Indians—without victories to compensate—exasperated men already at bitter odds over domestic questions. Almost inevitably John Robinson ascribed the martial misfortunes of Virginia to Dinwiddie. As the governor prepared to depart for home, Robinson denounced him as a military incompetent. Robinson did not know what person would succeed Dinwiddie. "God send it may be some body better acquainted with the unhappy business we have in hand," he wrote to George Washington. That young officer did not refrain from controversy with the governor, and at length Washington and Dinwiddie became enemies. Of their squabbles, in which the Virginian won no laurels, more later.

The vicissitudes of war induced Dinwiddie to reconsider the nature of the British colonial system and to propose reforms. It will be recalled that he had urged changes before he became governor in order to enhance the economic growth of the American colonies and their value to the mother country. He did not abandon his interest in such reforms. Thus, in 1756, he resurrected his scheme for a metallic currency to be used exclusively in the British colonies, and urged Lord Halifax and the Board of Trade to adopt it. Such money would supply a stable and much needed circulating medium. Colonial legislatures would have no further excuse for emitting cheap paper money in bewildering variety and for making it legal tender to the benefit of debtors at the expense of creditors. Parliament had already forbidden the New England colonies to attach legal tender quality to their paper currencies. Dinwiddie's scheme could have prevented monetary confusion, inflation, and abuse of creditors everywhere in British America. It was not seriously considered in London.

Not surprisingly, the veteran customs man also urged a change in the British laws regulating maritime commerce in order to strike at the French and to curb colonials who assisted them. American merchants less devoted to either the British empire or their own colonies than to personal profit traded with those enemies to the detriment of the war effort. Despite news of gunfire on the Ohio, American sea captains continued to carry provisions into French ports, or into neutral harbors from which such goods were transferred to French hands. Early in the struggle, Dinwiddie learned that vessels from New York City and Philadelphia conveyed large quantities of flour, bread, pork, beef, and vegetables to Louisbourg in exchange for sugar and molasses brought to that French fortress from French Caribbean islands.

Such traffic not only nourished the foe but narrowed the market for sugar and molasses produced in the British West Indies. Dinwiddie therefore pressed for a parliamentary act to require that all beef, pork, flour, bread, and "pease" exported from the North American colonies be carried only to British possessions. His remedy, never debated in the House of Commons, might have reduced traffic with the French; it would not have put a stop to the activities of the profit-seekers.

As the war progressed, the British navy struck hard at the French by checking the flow of reinforcements and supplies to Canada, Louisiana, and the possessions of Louis XV in the Caribbean Sea. However, merchants of Boston, New York,

Philadelphia, and other ports in the Thirteen Colonies managed by one subterfuge or another to send foodstuffs to Haiti and to Louisiana that strengthened the enemy.

As governor, however, Dinwiddie found the political defects in the British colonial system far more disturbing than its economic shortcomings. For it was ill contrived to wage war. Britain could not compel the American assemblies to raise money in the common cause or to mobilize even a large fraction of American manhood. Nor could troops and money when raised be put to the best use, because the several colonies were unable, even unwilling, to act in unison. British governors and American legislators often disagreed on measures; American lawmakers in one colony did not see eye-to-eye with those in neighboring provinces; and even British governors quarreled with each other.

The concentration of power in a few executives on the contrary gave the French—and the Spanish—an immense advantage in warfare in the New World. This, in large part, explains why the French, during several generations and despite the scantiness of men and means in their North American dominions, could mount offensives against the British colonies and instill fear in the Americans; why the French were so long able to cling to Canada and Louisiana; why a few hundreds of French soldiers, assisted by Indians, distance, and rugged terrain, could maintain themselves for so many years in Fort Duquesne. This also helps explain French successes in securing redskinned allies—no French Governor Glen urged savages to stay at home while a French Governor Dinwiddie was begging them to take up the tomahawk.

Dinwiddie was by no means the first man to see that disunity in the British empire in North America gravely hampered efforts to smite the French and Spanish. Again and again, in the latter part of the seventeenth century, and in the first half of the eighteenth, Englishmen familiar with the problems of empire had condemned its framework in North America and had offered remedies. They had earnestly pressed for increase in the authority of Whitehall and Westminster over the colonies, for the replacement of corporate and proprietary governments by royal ones, and for centralization of power within North

America through reduction of the number of colonies or by means of federation.

More than a score of schemes to attain those three goals, or part of them, had been put forward. Only one major effort had been made to translate such a scheme into reality—in the form of the Dominion of New England—and it had collapsed in consequence of colonial opposition and the Glorious Revolution of 1688, which drove its sponsor, King James II, into exile. In contrast to their interest in Europe, most London politicians knew very little about North America and cared not much more.

However, as the Seven Years' War approached and began, the desirability of reform in North America once more became apparent. Hence Dinwiddie's sponsor, the earl of Halifax, instigated action that led to the Albany Congress of 1754 and its plan of colonial federation. Hence the duke of Cumberland urged the sending of a viceroy to North America. As an advocate of change in the imperial structure on the western side of the Atlantic, Dinwiddie was by no means alone. His views somewhat resembled those of Benjamin Franklin of Pennsylvania, Thomas Hutchinson of Massachusetts, and other colonials. He put before his superiors in London various proposals for specific alterations and declared his desire for a general renovation of the imperial system.

The existence of the three proprietary colonies, Maryland, Delaware, and Pennsylvania, constituted a defect peculiarly vexing to Dinwiddie. The Calvert family looked upon Maryland primarily as a private estate, which ought to produce profit; the Penns similarly sought to extract income from their Pennsylvania and Delaware domains. The two clans, not much disposed to make unnecessary sacrifices in behalf of the British empire, were determined to prevent taxation of lands still in their hands. Both the Calverts and the Penns instructed governors appointed by them to veto tax measures that did not exempt their lands. On the other hand, the elected legislators of the three colonies seized the opportunity to be both patriotic and parsimonious. They virtuously voted levies for defense and at the same time made sure that these would not become law by insisting that the proprietors pay taxes on their lands. Even worse, from Dinwiddie's viewpoint, the Quakers, who were a minority in Pennsylvania but held a majority of the seats in its legislature, declined on principle to vote money to wage war in the early years of the struggle with the French. The Friends in that body continued to obstruct the war effort until threats from London persuaded many of them to retire to private life.

Before the beginning of the Seven Years' War Dinwiddie, not yet aware of the peculiarities of proprietary government, rather expected help from Maryland and Pennsylvania. He appealed to their governors for it. He hoped that the House of Delegates at Annapolis would "chearfully aid the intended expedition" against "the enemies of our country" at Fort Duquesne. "I expect aid" from Pennsylvania, he wrote to the governor of that colony.

But he soon learned to doubt that either Maryland or Pennsylvania would act. They "do nothing," he wrote to James Abercromby in June 1754. They shared a "lethargic stupidity" that permeated the colonies, he repoted to Lord Halifax in a letter of July. "It's a pity," he declared in the following January, that clash between the governor and legislators of Pennsylvania should prevent that colony from raising even £20,000 to support the Braddock expedition. In the early spring of 1755 he had to report that the burgesses were reluctant to vote money for that purpose because they would be "dupes" to do so when other colonies were "indolent and passive." If the colonies would act "as one man," they could easily drive back the French. Pennsylvania, "the richest and most populous province" of George II in North America, in Dinwiddie's opinion, had "at last condescended to supply us with some flour."

Thoroughly disgusted by the inactivity of Maryland and Pennsylvania, he officially condemned their behavior as "monstrously" backward in April of that year. In a private letter to Lord Halifax he urged that the crown purchase the rights of the Penns and Calverts and turn Maryland and Pennsylvania into royal colonies, at least that royal authority over the two somehow be firmly established. In August he declared to Governor Arthur Dobbs of North Carolina that the proprietary governments were obstacles in "all our affairs" and that they

would continue to be such until Parliament intervened and reduced them "to a proper obedience to the King's commands."

In October, in the sad wake of Braddock's defeat, he came
forth flatly with a denunciation of the "shameful" behavior of
the two colonies and formally urged on his superiors in London the necessity of altering their political institutions. He also
pressed Robert Hunter Morris, who was considering resignation as governor of Pennsylvania and a journey to England, to
exert his personal influence toward the same end.

Dinwiddie continued to complain in public letter after private letter to London about the behavior of the proprietary
colonies. In May 1756 he again ardently urged that they be re-
formed. After William Pitt had become the principal figure in
the British ministry, Dinwiddie tried to persuade the Great
Commoner, in June 1757, to act. His pleadings were all in vain
—and so were later recommendations from Benjamin Franklin
and other enemies of the Penns and Calverts. Those families
continued to enjoy their estates and to quarrel with the inhabitants of their colonies until their political rights were extin-
guished by the American Revolution.

The replacement of proprietary officers by royal ones
would have reduced internal friction in Pennsylvania and
Maryland that injured the British war effort. But it would not
have put an end to the squabbling, as Dinwiddie learned from
less than joyous experience. A royal dominion Virginia might
be; but the House of Burgesses did not therefore immediately
respond to every royal wish or command. Dinwiddie again
and again condemned the Virginians because they did not uni-
formly and eagerly take up arms against the French and Indians. Nor was he satisfied that Virginia had made sufficient
financial sacrifices on every occasion. Nevertheless, during his
tenure of office Virginia supplied about £200,000 sterling
toward carrying on the struggle. The citizens of the Old Dominion were taxed as never before in order to raise that sum.
Accordingly, Dinwiddie, considering the record, also frequently praised Virginia in his reports to London for generous
financial support of the British war effort.

Moreover, royal governors as well as proprietary governors
did not invariably see eye-to-eye and toil hand-in-hand; witness the short-sighted conduct of James Glen. A collection of

royal colonies could not efficiently and simultaneously raise men and money to defend themselves, much less to wage offensive war. Accordingly, Dinwiddie felt by no means certain that taking away the political rights of the proprietors would remove every obstacle to the British war effort. On the contrary, he urged various other measures—and endorsed still more which he did not originate— to increase the might of the armed forces in North America.

Most of those measures entailed greater exertion of British authority over the colonies. He did not want in the colonies a representative of the crown similar to a Spanish viceroy. He was no believer in Romanov or Bourbon autocracy. But he could not conceive of massive concentration of political power in the hands of the American colonists. They—at least the majority of them—did not desire it. Besides, he was in no way an American; it became increasingly obvious to him that the crown and Parliament must assert sway over the British possessions in North America as never before.

All the same, Dinwiddie favored colonial combination. Indeed, in 1753 he sent Lord Halifax a scheme for creating two confederacies, one northern and one southern. He believed that it would be easier to hold regular meetings of commissioners in two regions than in one and that "the affairs of each district" would be "more concisely enquired into, and easier regulated" by two councils.

Hence it was, in part, that he played a less than ardent role in the drive toward centralization that led to the Albany Congress in 1754 and its plan of union. Instructed by the Board of Trade to do what he could to induce Virginia to send delegates to Albany, he expressed no profound regret because the burgesses declined to act. They declared that Virginia money and energy must be devoted to the defense of the colony. He expressed the hope that those excuses would be acceptable in London—and was reprimanded from London for his lack of zeal. Dinwiddie was not satisfied with the Albany Plan. He preferred his own scheme, which he believed to be "more reasonable and more constitutional." Examining the Albany document, he saw "some articles in it of an extraordinary nature." In particular, he feared that it would invest too large powers in the British-appointed president who was to serve as the head of the American general council. He cautiously refrained from making official comment on the plan, however, as he wished to avoid a clash of opinion with his superiors.

Remaining convinced that some sort of colonial "junction" was "by all means necessary and proper," the governor clung for many months to his own scheme. However, he wrote to Halifax in November 1754 that he would bow to His Lordship's "more superior" judgment. At the end of April in the following year he announced that he had adopted the opinion of Halifax and the Board of Trade, that a "union of all the colonies is greatly to be desired." He shared their disappointment when it became apparent that the Albany Plan was disliked in the colonies and that the British ministry was not eager to establish a colonial confederacy.

Dinwiddie concluded that the Americans would never establish "a proper union" for their common protection without the intervention of Parliament. By February 1756 he had abandoned hope that action would soon be taken. Nevertheless, he continued to believe that decisive measures should be adopted by Britain to reform the empire in North America. In one of his last reports as governor, a letter of June 1757, to William Pitt, Dinwiddie urged military necessity as an impelling reason not only for royalizing all of His Majesty's colonies in North America but for forming them into "a coalition."

But Dinwiddie believed that even those changes were not sufficient to put Britain's North American empire in order. For he doubted that a federal council would steadily raise enough money to defend the colonies—he assumed that they would be faced by formidable enemies for many years to come. Britain must see to it that the money was forthcoming. The money must be extracted from American pockets, since Britain was already contributing heavily for defense, and the colonists could well afford to shoulder somewhat heavier financial burdens.

Accordingly, he proposed that Parliament compel them to contribute. As early as June 1754 he officially suggested to Sir Thomas Robinson, secretary of state in special charge of American business, that the British legislature should "oblige" each of the colonies to raise its fair share of money, by a poll tax of one shilling, "or otherways." He sent the same recommendation to the Board of Trade. He showed no concern that such action by Parliament might be denounced by the Americans as unconstitutional. Indeed, he believed it desirable for Britain to "take some proper course to bring all the colonies into proper sense of their duty."

In the following month, trying to raise troops to move against Fort Duquesne, he sharpened his proposal. Parliament ought to enact "a general poll tax" of a half-crown sterling, he asserted in letters to Robinson, Secretary at War Henry Fox, Lord Halifax, Earl Granville, and the Board of Trade. In September he again officially and unofficially pressed for a parliamentary head tax in letters sent to London.

He was "fully convinc'd nothing can be done, or any expedition conducted in these parts, with a dependence on the assemblies" for money. The members of those bodies were infatuated, perverse, and lethargic. He said that "the people in these colonies seem adverse to every thing . . . for the service of the Crown or their own good." An act of Parliament was needed "to reclaim them to their duty to the best of Kings," and for their own preservation. At that time he entertained hope that the British ministry would ask Parliament to impose the tax.

Dinwiddie continued to plead for parliamentary taxation of the colonists to support military forces for their defense. He repeated that it was necessary in a letter to Lord Halifax of February 1755, At the close of the following April he again urged it in reports sent to Robinson and Halifax. "An union of the colonies is greatly to be desired," he wrote to his patron, "but even then these colonies will continue obstinate and fractious, unless a general tax is laid on all the colonies by a British act of Parliament."

Pressing for a levy on the colonists by the British legislature, Dinwiddie at first justified it on the score of military emergency, then on the added ground that it was desirable in order to assert the authority of the mother country. He went further. Asked by the Board of Trade for detailed advice regarding defense of the northern colonies and the associated problems of relations with the Indians, he offered proposals, in

LAKE ERIE

NEW YORK

Creek

★ Fort Le Boeuf
(Waterford)

French

Allegheny River

OHIO

Venango
(Franklin)

*George
Washington's
Western
Travels*

1753-1754

Beaver River

Allegheny River

Ohio R.

Logstown (Economy)

Pittsburgh

Fort Du Quesne
Braddock's Field
Queen Alliquippas

Shannopin's Town
Fraziers

WEST VIRGINIA

Youghiogheny River

Laurel Hill

Shawnese Cabins

Réas Town
(Bedford)

Gist's (Mt. Braddock)
Half King's Rocks
Jumonville's Camp
Fort Necessity

Turkey Foot
(Confluence)

1758

1754

MARYLAND

Wills' Creek
(Cumberland)

1755

Potomac R.

1753-1754 ············
1754 ××××××××××××
1755 ============
1758 – – – – – – –

Scale of Miles

0   10   20   30   40   50

Washington's western travels. Routes taken by George Washington in his several courier trips and military campaigns in the Ohio country.

February 1756, for permanent arrangements that included British taxation of the Americans.

The governor based these proposals on the assumption that the French would be driven back to the St. Lawrence, but would remain in control of Canada as well as of New Orleans and its vicinity. British territory would extend to the Mississippi and at least as far to the northwest as the village of Detroit, all that wide region being "indisputably" the property of the British crown—his definition of the rights of Britain in North America expanded after 1753.

To protect the colonies against renewed French aggression, he urged that eleven forts be erected and maintained "at the extremes of the lands" of Great Britain. A total of 1,850 men would be needed for garrison service. He hoped that friendly Indians would help to build or rebuild the posts. He suggested that convicts transported across the Atlantic, "unhappy wretches," serve their sentences in labor on the forts and that they be given adjacent lands on which to settle when they were set free.

Toward winning the affection of the Indians, he proposed that two blacksmiths be stationed at every fort to mend their guns and that one schoolmaster be assigned to every post to teach English and morality to the Indian young, and "to give them a true notion of the Supreme God." Also to reduce unrest among the redmen, he would try to impose rigid controls on the whites who bartered with them, "the most abandon'd wretches in the world." To achieve that end, he would establish a board of commissioners in every colony to oversee the activities of the traders.

Further to provide for the defense of the American settlements, he suggested the formation of a new colony beyond the Appalachian divide, to be peopled by foreign Protestants as well as natural subjects of the crown. Thus the menace of Indian attacks would be pushed away from the existing frontiers of Virginia and her neighbors.

Dinwiddie believed, and not without reason, that money for such purposes could not be got from the assemblies of the several American colonies. Therefore, since the mother country had incurred "great expense . . . to protect and defend them," Parliament should levy a temporary poll tax of twelve pence per annum on all Americans for two years to pay for building the forts. To maintain them and to meet other expenses engendered by his proposals, Parliament should impose a permanent tax, after the expiration of twenty-four months, of two shillings on every one hundred acres of American land. He favored such a levy because it would be "chiefly paid by people of the greatest property and great land holders." He observed that it would be much less than that exacted by Parliament from British owners of soil. "I know our people will be inflam'd if they hear of my . . . proposal, as they are averse to all taxes," he wrote. Nevertheless, said he, such a levy was necessary and proper.

Obviously Governor Dinwiddie, though well aware of American resistance to royal authority, did not see far into the future. He failed to perceive that British garrisons in forts in the American wilderness would be gravely exposed to Indian attack—a fact that General Sir Jeffery Amherst would later learn to his sorrow. Recognizing that parliamentary taxation to support those garrisons would "inflame" the Virginians, he did not envisage massive American revolt against novel taxation for revenue. Recommending additional restrictions on American commerce, he was not aware that such crampings would enormously increase colonial discontent. He advocated several of the measures, in principle if not in detail, that provoked American rebellion in and after 1765,

Dinwiddie's outlook was, not surprisingly, that of a man committed by birth and by office to the "metropolis" of the empire. It may be suggested that his proposals were offered before the destruction of the French strongholds in North America greatly altered the relationship between the mother country and the colonists, that he could not take that change into account. But it is true that, after his return to England, when the French were about to cede Canada and eastern Louisiana to Britain, he remained of the same imperialist cast of mind.

Did the reports and urgings of Governor Dinwiddie affect the making of policy in London regarding government of the empire? They doubtless contributed somewhat to a growing conviction in the imperial capital that Britain must assert firmer control over the colonies, and that the colonists ought to assume a larger share of the financial burdens of empire.

The governor had more to do with one specific change in imperial structure. It was his plea for direction of the military effort in Virginia by a veteran British army officer that primarily led to the appointment of Edward Braddock as commander in chief. That plea may also have exercised minor influence in the selection of the earl of Loudoun for the same post in 1756. The office of commander in chief of the British forces in North America persisted beyond the Seven Years' War, and its holder became a major personage in the imperial hierarchy in North America, thanks in part to the impetus supplied by Dinwiddie.

Chapter 7
Dinwiddie and Washington

George Washington was not only a majestic hero, but one almost without fault. He quarreled with Dinwiddie. Therefore, Dinwiddie was in the wrong. So said Jared Sparks, Francis Parkman, and other American historians of the nineteenth and twentieth centuries. More objective scholars have urged that the towering Virginian was inevitably less than divine. Great and good men have often engaged in hot dispute with each other; those who wrangled with Washington were not necessarily weak or wicked. Certain it is that the governor befriended young Washington, that the two continued to enjoy cordial relations during many months under most trying circumstances, and that they at last turned against each other. It will not do to argue that Dinwiddie was entirely at fault. Indeed, the older man exhibited a graciousness that was not reciprocated by the young officer; he said farewell to Washington like a gentleman.

Precisely when Dinwiddie and Washington first met cannot be ascertained; their acquaintance began as early as January 1752. Returning from a journey to Barbados with his older half-brother Lawrence, undertaken in a vain effort to improve Lawrence's health, Washington delivered letters to Dinwiddie at Williamsburg and was invited to dinner by the governor. The following June Washington applied to Dinwiddie for an appointment as one of four adjutants entrusted with the task of supervising the training of militiamen in four parts of Virginia. Then only 21 years of age, he got the job and the rank of major but not the territory he wanted. It may reasonably be inferred that Lawrence Washington's father-in-law, William Fairfax—representative of Lord Fairfax in Virginia, member of the British customs service, and holder of a seat in the Virginia Council—had some influence on Dinwiddie's decision. The governor did what he could to please the powerful Fairfax clan. Later, he gave Washington the district that the major desired, the Northern Neck of Virginia.

If the governor tried to satisfy important people, he did not knowingly select incompetents for office; nor did he maintain such men in their places to placate their powerful relatives or friends. He was a good judge of men, and no doubt discerned splendid qualities in Washington. He certainly placed great faith in him in 1753 when he sent the new adjutant out to the Ohio to demand that the French withdraw to Canada. When the youthful major returned to Williamsburg from that mission, Dinwiddie received him with pleasure, for he had been "in some pain" lest harm had come to Washington. The governor then, in January 1754, entrusted the major with the far greater responsibility of leading forth militia to check the advance of the French.

When the burgesses undertook to raise a regiment to serve against the French, Dinwiddie placed Colonel Joshua Fry in command of it, in the following March. An Englishman who had taught mathematics at the College of William and Mary, Fry presumably had some knowledge of engineering that would be useful in building and reducing forts. It was obviously no slight to Washington to be placed under Fry. He solicited an appointment as lieutenant colonel, indicated eagerness to serve under Fry, and expressed a desire to learn more about the military art. On receiving his promotion he wrote to Dinwiddie, "I hope my future behaviour will sufficiently testify the true sense I have of this kindness." He had another small reason for being grateful to the governor. He was permitted as adjutant—with the other men holding that office—to draw his salary of £100 per annum, to hire a deputy at a lower salary to perform his duties, and to pocket the difference.

As Washington moved forward to the Ohio in the spring of that year, he and other officers became seriously discontented. They were dissatisfied with their pay and perquisites, not because of niggardliness on the part of Dinwiddie, but because of the parsimony of the committee led by John Robinson that controlled Virginia expenditures. They complained to the governor. Washington asked Dinwiddie to be allowed to act as a volunteer without pay rather than to serve under the terms imposed by the committee.

The governor undertook to remove the legitimate grievancs of the officers; pointed out that others were without substance; and adjured Washington to see to it that his officers did their duty. Washington should employ his "usual good sense" in pacifying his subordinates. He chided Washington. He felt "concern and surprize to find a gent. whom I particularly consider'd, and from whom I had so great" expectations, "appear so differently from himself." The young officer was not permitted to resign.

Washington responded:

I am much concern'd, that your Honour should seem to charge me with ingratitude for your generous, and my indeserved favours . . . nothing is a greater stranger to my breast, or a sin that my soul abhors, than the black and detestable one ingratitude. I retain a true sense of your kindness, and want nothing but opportunity to give testimony of my willingness to oblige you, as far as my life and fortune extend.

He continued, unsuccessfully, to ask for himself and his fellow officers rewards equivalent to those given to British officers of the same ranks, but he also persuaded his subordinates that they must accept less, for the time being.

The death of Colonel Fry at the end of May forced Dinwiddie to choose a new commander of the expedition moving toward the Ohio. Mindful of the energy that Washington had displayed in the first clash with the French, the governor promoted him to the command of the Virginia regiment with the rank of colonel. However, he found it prudent to put the young colonel, together with British officers of the independent regulars taking the field, under the leadership of James Innes, whom he commissioned as colonel and commander in chief.

Redcoated captains, unwilling in the past to take orders

from a mere militiaman, could not so easily claim that Innes was their military inferior; he had served as a royal officer in the British attack on Cartagena. It will be recalled that he was a close friend of Dinwiddie, who placed great faith in him and praised him for bravery, industry, and honesty. Washington was much pleased by the arrangement cleverly devised by Dinwiddie. He wrote to the governor,

"I rejoice that I am likely to be happy under the command of a superior officer and man of sense, it is what I have ardently wish'd for. I shall here beg leave to return my grateful thanks for your favour in promoting me to the command of the regiment, believe me, Hon'ble Sir, when I assure you my breast is warm'd with every generous sentiment that your goodness can inspire; I want nothing but opportunity to testifie my sincere regard for your person, to whom I stand indebted for so many unmerited favours."

It is apparent that Dinwiddie had done all that he could for Washington and that Washington was well aware of the fact. But the governor could not satisfy planter Landon Carter, who had more than his share of jaundice, that he had done justice to the young officer. Carter suspected that Dinwiddie favored his "darling" Innes because Innes was a Scot and because he would protect an important economic interest of the governor. No good reason exists to believe either of Carter's allegations.

Washington's defeat and humiliation at Fort Necessity did not turn Dinwiddie against him. Others censured Washington, in particular because the articles of capitulation he had signed admitted responsibility for *"l'assassinat"* of Jumonville. (Washington defended his signature on the ground that he did not know, because of his ignorance of French, that he had acknowledged guilt for a political murder.) But Dinwiddie, in dispatches and private letters sent to London and Paris, praised Washington for displaying good judgment and bravery. In one private letter, to Lord Halifax, he did remark that he had ordered Washington to remain in camp until all his forces were available. He insisted that Washington had not intended to plead guilty to assassination of Jumonville. He informed Washington that he continued to rely upon his "former and usual diligence and spirit."

But the Dinwiddie-Washington honeymoon came to an end. The governor's efforts to prevent strife between the officers of the Virginia regiment and those of the independent regulars had failed. The redcoats positively declined to recognize Virginia commissions as equivalents of their own royal appointments. Redcoated Captain James Mackay would not take orders from Lieutenant Colonel Washington. He and other British officers went unrebuked by the home government for impudence or disobedience. There was grave doubt in London that professional military men should be subject to the commands of mere militia officers.

It will be recalled that Dinwiddie attempted to get British status for the Virginia regiment in order to secure harmony and gain efficiency on campaign. In October 1754 he suggested in letters to London that it be made part of the British army; that he be appointed as its colonel; and that he be authorized to select its officers, none of them to be given rank above that of captain. A local precedent of sorts could be found for his proposals: Governor William Gooch had served as a colonel of such a regiment in the British attack on Cartagena.

Dinwiddie had no intention of leading the Virginians into battle; after all, many colonels in the British army exerted little energy militarily beyond the collection of their emoluments. Dinwiddie claimed that the Virginia officers would be "greatly pleased" to serve under his nominal command. He expressed belief that they would also be content with their new royal commissions, even though none of them would hold rank higher than that of captain. He indicated that his scheme was "absolutely necessary to confirm peace among the officers." Dinwiddie realized that James Innes would hardly be content with a captaincy, but he assured Innes that his interests would be protected. He did not insist upon a colonelcy for himself; he was prepared to act in behalf of His Majesty George II in any way the British ministry thought proper.

Informed of Dinwiddie's scheme, most of the Virginia officers told the governor that they were prepared to accept him as their colonel and to take royal commissions. A lieutenancy in the British army was far more valuable than one in colonial forces. Normally, a British officer had to buy his first commission and all others up to the level of colonel. The commission was usually considered a piece of property, and it could be sold. Besides, he could continue to draw half pay after the crown no longer required his services. A captaincy was, of course, worth more than a lieutenancy. Besides, a commission in the royal forces opened the prospect of a military career with rewards more certain and substantial than those of a colonial officer. However, Innes seems to have been unhappy. Certainly, Washington rejected the scheme.

No evidence has been found to indicate that Washington objected to service under Dinwiddie. However, he treated with contempt the suggestion that he accept a royal captaincy. His pride was injured. Were he to accept a new British captaincy, he would be junior to all the captains of the independent regulars. "I think," he wrote, "the disparity between the present offer of a company, and my former rank, too great to expect any real satisfaction or enjoyment in a corps, where I once did, or thought I had a right to, command." He could not bear the thought that "every captain, bearing the King's commission, every half-pay officer, or other, appearing with such a commission, would rank before me." He suspected that Dinwiddie's plan had been inspired by an officer or officers of the independent regulars; he was erroneously informed that it had received sanction from London. He resigned his colonelcy. He also spurned an arrangement that would have permitted him to retain his Virginia rank while serving as a British captain.

In November Dinwiddie again urged that the home government adopt his scheme. Mentioning that Washington had retired to private life because of dispute over rank, he now recommended Innes for a majority in the proposed regiment, and he asked for authority to select another officer of the same rank. Probably he hoped to induce Washington to serve as a major junior to Innes. He requested James Abercromby to do what he could in London to secure the establishment of the royal regiment, but not to press hard in behalf of the governor for its colonelcy.

In February 1755 Dinwiddie, aware that his plan for a royal Virginia regiment had been set aside in London and that General Braddock was enroute to Virginia, assured Innes that

his services would be properly recognized and that Dinwiddie
would urge the general to offer Innes some sort of preferment.
Innes nevertheless decided to resign. The governor "strongly
recommended" him to Braddock. Braddock apparently promised Innes that he would write to London in his behalf; but
Innes failed to secure a new royal commission. He ultimately
accepted command of Fort Cumberland.

Did Dinwiddie also enlarge upon Washington's merits to
the general? Evidence is lacking that he did so. In March 1755,
in a private letter to William Allen of Philadelphia, despite his
earlier defenses of Washington's behavior at Fort Necessity,
he indicated that "Washington's conduct was in many steps
wrong, and did not conform to his orders from me, or he had
not engaged till the other forces had joined him."

On the other hand, it seems quite unlikely that Dinwiddie
spoke to the general against the young Virginian. Washington
indicated a desire to be allowed to serve on Braddock's staff
as a volunteer. His wish granted, he served in the Braddock
campaign as an aide-de-camp without commission. After this
arrangement was made, Braddock considered the possibility
of appointing Washington as a royal captain. He informed
Washington that he lacked power to grant a higher commission. Washington continued to believe that he deserved more
than a British captaincy.

Before he took the field, Washington suggested in a letter
to William Fairfax that he considered Dinwiddie to be less
than a great man. He met several governors who had come to
Alexandria to confer with Braddock. He was "well receiv'd
by them all," especially William Shirley of Massachusetts,
"whose character, and appearance has perfectly charm'd me,
as I think every word and every action discovers the gent'n
and great politician. I heartily wish something of such una-
nimity amongst us, as appear'd to reign between him and his
assembly." Early in June, in another letter to Fairfax, he commented, contemptuously, that "General Innis has accepted of
a commission to be governour of Cumberland Fort, where
he is to reside, and will shortly receive another to be hang-
man, or something of that kind."

The great gallantry displayed by Washington in the battle
of the Monongahela and subsequent events brought a restora-

tion of friendship between the young Virginia and the aging
Dinwiddie. Washington sent a report concerning the disastrous defeat to the governor, who responded with a letter to
"Dear Washington" congratulating him on his splendid performance.

In August, recuperating at Mount Vernon, Washington
concluded that his military career had been most unprofitable:
He had been defeated at Fort Necessity, had lost his military
equipment in the campaign of 1754, and "had my commission
taken from me or, in other words my com'd reduced under
pretence of an order from home." (He still believed that the
Dinwiddie plan to turn the Virginia regiment into a royal
one grew out of a conspiracy directed against him and other
officers of the Old Dominion.) He had again lost his military
gear in the unsuccessful campaign with Braddock.

Washington was nevertheless willing to resume leadership
of the troops that must defend Virginia frontiers, if that "command is press'd upon me by the genl. voice of the country,
and offer'd upon such terms as can't be objected against." If
honor required him to defend his personal rights, it also demanded that he serve in time of emergency. The Virginia
assembly gave him £300 as a reward for his services and
losses of equipment in Braddock's defeat. Dinwiddie did indeed ask him to resume service as a colonel and commander
in chief of the Virginia forces on the western frontiers. There
was another candidate—Innes?—who ardently sought the
post, but the governor wanted Washington.

Washington agreed to accept it; he was needed. Along with
his commission, dated August 15, he received authority to
appoint all the officers who would serve under him. Dinwiddie
already knew that two companies of the independent regulars
were going to Pennsylvania and shortly learned that all of
them were leaving Virginia. It may be that Washington's
scruples about going back into military service were removed,
or reduced, by assurances from Dinwiddie that he would not
again be vexed by claims to command put forward by the captains of those companies.

Did Dinwiddie also tell Washington that he would again
propose him for a royal commission? Probably he did. Certainly Washington knew as early as the beginning of Novem-

ber that the governor had written London to secure such a commission for him. On September 7, in a letter to Sir Thomas Robinson, Dinwiddie warmly urged that royal commissions be granted to Washington and to his officers. Washington, he wrote, "I think a man of great merit and resolution," and Braddock, had the general lived long enough, would surely have recommended Washington to the royal favor. He repeated his request in a private letter to Lord Halifax.

Dinwiddie also pressed James Abercromby to solicit in London in behalf of the Virginia officers. He asked for blank commissions, which he could complete. He no longer sought military rank for himself; indeed, he rather expected to be replaced by a soldier. He wanted brevet commissions for the Virginians. Under such an arrangement Washington would become a British colonel on Virginia pay. In a November letter to Robinson, Dinwiddie again tried to exert influence in behalf of the Virginia officers. Washington heard a rumor that same month that the commissions were en route from England, but gave it no credit. They did not come.

Before Dinwiddie could secure an answer to those urgings, a new dispute over rank developed between Washington and Captain John Dagworthy of Maryland. The command of Fort Cumberland had been temporarily consigned by James Innes to Virginian Adam Stephen who had casually conveyed it to Dagworthy. Zealously executing his duties, Washington was confronted by an officer who not only refused to obey his orders, but even declined to let Washington take Virginia supplies from a fort erected by Virginians with Virginia money. Dagworthy, once the holder of a royal commission, had been on halfpay, had sold his halfpay, and was only a Maryland captain. Nevertheless, because he had once been the king's officer and because he presided over a fort located in Maryland, he scorned commands from Washington.

Dagworthy's behavior exasperated Washington and his officers. In consequence, Dinwiddie tried to provide for them, at least temporarily, by another device. Could not General Shirley grant brevet commissions? He entreated Shirley to give such appointments to three Virginia officers, including a colonelcy for Washington. But Shirley would not, perhaps could not, give his consent to the proposal. He merely instructed Governor Horatio Sharpe to bring his troublesome subordinate to reason; and Sharpe declined to put Dagworthy in his proper place.

Thereupon the officers of the Virginia regiment formally petitioned Shirley for British rank. Washington informed Dinwiddie that he would "resign a commission, which you were generously pleased to offer me, (and for which I shall always retain a grateful sense of the favor)" rather than submit to the pretensions of Dagworthy. He asked Dinwiddie for leave to go north to present the case of the Virginians in person to Shirley. The governor agreed, and again urged the general to comply—to no avail.

Shirley no doubt treated Washington as graciously in Boston in February 1756 as he had in Alexandria in the spring of 1755. But he did no more than issue an order requiring Dagworthy to obey commands from Washington when the Virginian happened to be at Fort Cumberland. Washington unhappily turned southward. "I have learned," Adam Stephen wrote him, "that you have been a long journey, purely to pay your compliments, and hear some handsome things, which one is always to expect from persons conversant at the courts of princes, and especially from one who has resided so long at Paris the metropolis of a polite nation." Stephen was also disappointed.

Washington "went to Williamsburgh fully resolved to resign my commission, but was diswaded from it at least for a time." It may well be that Dinwiddie begged him not to abandon hope of British preferment in consequence of the pleas for it sent to London by the governor. Besides, another prospect was opening for Washington, an appointment as second-in-command to Governor Sharpe in the expedition planned for that year against Fort Duquesne. Sharpe recommended him to Shirley for a royal commission in that post. But Shirley, about to be replaced, replied that he doubted his authority to give Washington the rank he desired. He promised to urge the appointment to the earl of Loudoun, who would soon succeed him. But the plan for the expedition was set aside in the meantime and Washington returned to his arduous tasks of frontier defense.

Dinwiddie received discouraging news from England. A

letter to James Abercromby in January 1756 expressed his fear that the blank commissions he "so earnestly desired" would be consigned to the British commander in chief in North America—and that officer would probably give them to his friends and the friends of his friends rather than to Virginians. Soon after Washington returned to the Virginia outposts both he and his subordinates complained about their lot. His officers sent letters emphasizing their sacrifices and accusing government of ingratitude. On the other hand, critics in Williamsburg, including members of the House of Burgesses, condemned the Virginia troops for idleness, drunkenness, gambling, swearing, and inattention to duty. Discontent increased as the result of a fight with the Indians in which Captain John Mercer was slain. Washington continued to be unhappy.

Dinwiddie tried to encourage the young colonel. In a letter of April 23 he acceded to a request from Washington that a commission as lieutenant be given to a brother of Washington, and adjured him to "keep up your spirits." He also conveyed to Washington a report that Generals Lord Loudoun and James Abercromby were en route to America and that "His Majesty intends to send blank commissions for the Americans." If the news proved to be true, "I doubt not you will be taken care of," he said.

In May 1756 the Virginia Assembly, obviously with Dinwiddie's endorsement, added its efforts to those of the governor in behalf of the officers of the Old Dominion. He sent the legislators' memorial to the crown across the ocean without comment. However, John Robinson shared the expectation of Dinwiddie that Loudoun would satisfy the officers before the memorial could be considered in London. Wrote William Fairfax to Washington on May 9, "The Governor thinks you will and perhaps the regiment be put on the English or Irish establishment." Washington asked Dinwiddie to recommend him to Loudoun. The governor needed no prodding.

Informed that Loudoun was authorized to raise royal troops in North America, Dinwiddie once more took up his vigorous pen in behalf of Washington, He had not yet made the acquaintance of Loudoun, but he was a "particular friend" of his second in command, Abercromby. Dinwiddie therefore, before the end of June, begged Abercromby to exert his interest with the new commander in chief in favor of

"Colonel George Washington, who, I will venture to say, is a very deserving gentleman, and has from the beginning commanded the forces of this dominion. Gen'l Braddock had so high an esteem for his merit that he made him one of his aide-de-camps, and if he had surviv'd I believe he would have provided handsomely for him in the regulars. He is a person much beloved here and has gone through many hardships in the service, and I really think he has great merit, and believe he can raise more men here than any one present that I know. If his Lordship will be so kind as to promote him in the British establishment I think he will answer my recommendation."

Just what rank Dinwiddie sought for Washington he did not say. But he could not have expected to get a full British colonelcy, with all its emoluments, for the Virginian.

Then came bad news from England for Washington, and for Dinwiddie. The governor learned that the British cabinet, with the consent of Parliament, intended to raise troops in America but to place them substantially under European officers and to concentrate on the enlistment of German colonists. His pleas sent to London in behalf of Washington and his fellow officers had been in vain. Surely, he protested in disappointment to agent James Abercromby, the experienced and well qualified Virginia officers ought to have been preferred to foreigners. Nor was his application through General Abercromby to Loudoun in favor of Washington heeded. Loudoun had been ordered to raise a regiment of four battalions and had been appointed as its colonel. He offered no place in it to Washington.

Dinwiddie did not bother to recommend to Abercromby or to Loudoun the incorporation of the Virginia troops into the British forces. It was obvious that the commander in chief would not be interested in such a proposal. When the officers of the Virginia regiment, pursuing their goal of royal commissions, sent a memorial to Loudoun to express their wishes, Dinwiddie and the Council declined to endorse it. Washington sent the paper on to Beverley Robinson in New York, who conveyed it to an aide-de-camp of Loudoun. The general considered it, and promised an early answer. But he did not act.

The governor also at last began to turn against his military commander. In August he informed Washington that "I shall be glad you were here about the 20th Nov'r, when I expect the Earl of Loudon." Obviously, Dinwiddie then was still willing to give the colonel an opportunity to place his claims to British preferment before the general at Williamsburg. But all the governor's efforts in championship of Washington had been in vain; and he had reason to believe that it was idle to continue them.

Besides, the two men both burdened by heavy responsibilities almost beyond their powers were again drifting apart. They could see no way to put a decisive end to the Indian raids into the valley of the Shenandoah. In failing health, Dinwiddie found his duties to be increasingly onerous. He wished to return to England. Washington was bedeviled, not only by hostile redmen, but also by discontent among his officers and men. He could hardly preserve discipline. His hopes for a military career were jeopardized.

In May 1756 Washington began to complain to Dinwiddie that he was not sufficiently instructed so that he could execute his duties. He voiced that grievance, not only to the governor, but to William Fairfax and John Robinson. Fairfax suggested to Washington that Dinwiddie's seeming "omission or neglect may proceed from the confidence entertaind of your ability and discretion." Whereas Fairfax tried to soothe the colonel, Robinson doubtless welcomed the complaint Washington made in August that "in all important matters I am directed in this ambiguous and uncertain way." He did not seek to pour oil upon troubled water.

Corresponding of necessity with Robinson about money for his command, Washington also discussed military policy with the speaker, not to the credit of Dinwiddie. During the campaign of 1756 the governor and the colonel debated extensively whether or not Fort Cumberland should be abandoned by Virginia troops. Washington wished to concentrate his men south of the fort. Dinwiddie believed that it would be unwise to desert it. Loudoun eventually settled the dispute, ordering that the post be maintained.

In the autumn relations between the two men became tense. On the third day of September the *Virginia Gazette* published an extraordinary essay entitled "The Virginia-Centinel No. X" signed "L & V." The author or authors remain unknown. The essay wittily and savagely attacked the Virginia regiment. Its officers were incompetent and brutal. It was composed of "dastardly debauchees" who spent their time "skulking in forts."

The scurrilous piece condemned Dinwiddie by implication; but its barbs were aimed directly at Washington. He threatened in private letters to resign. But friends assured him that his reputation was too splendid to be injured by nasty calumny. Augustine Washington, his half brother, visited Williamsburg to assess the situation. He reported to Washington that the colonel was "in as great esteem as ever with the Govr. here & especially the house of Burgesses," that John Robinson and other friends of Washington were utterly opposed to his resignation. If Washington left the service of Virginia, they feared that James Innes would succeed him, to the displeasure of all in Virginia, "a few Scotchmen excepted." Washington ought at least to wait until the British government should respond to the memorial sent to London by the House of Burgesses in behalf of his regiment, until Washington had had an opportunity to speak for himself to Lord Loudoun.

In November Washington's officers, claiming that Dinwiddie and the burgesses had neglected to defend them against unjustified castigation by "The Virginia Centinel," formally declared as a body that, without redress, they would abandon the service of the colony. But John Robinson warmly urged Washington not to quit his command because of an attack by a "vile and ignorant scribbler," and the storm blew over. Just before Christmas Washington assured the speaker that he would remain in service until he should have an opportunity to see Loudoun. He again found fault with Dinwiddie: "My orders are dark, doubtful, and uncertain; *to-day approved, to-morrow condemned*." Regarding his performance and that of Dinwiddie, Richard Bland sent astute comment to Washington. The troubles of Virginia could not fairly be ascribed to either the governor or the colonel. They arose in large part from the conduct of the House of Burgesses. From the beginning of hostilities the burgesses had supplied too little money, in dibs and dabs, for the war effort.

Dinwiddie at length ceased to recommend Washington. Did he definitely turn against him in November 1756? At that time, urging Loudoun to send a force of Pennsylvanians, Marylanders, and Virginians against Fort Duquesne in the next campaign, he told Loudoun that "good officers to command will be wanting." He did not specifically propose Washington for an appointment. On December 15 the governor responded to recommendations from Washington and from Colonel George William Fairfax that he appoint as commissaries for the Virginia regiment William Ramsay, a relative of Washington by marriage, and Dr. Thomas Carlyle, brother-in-law of Fairfax. Dinwiddie, consulting the Council, refused their request.

However, informed that Loudoun would be at Williamsburg in January, he also wrote to Washington, "When he arrives I shall give you notice of it." Two days after Christmas he confirmed the leave he had given Washington to see the general in Williamsburg, "as you will be able to give him a good acc't of our back country." Thus he continued to make it possible for the young Virginian to press his claims before the general until the year 1756 was almost ended.

Loudoun decided, however, not to visit Williamsburg, but to hold meetings with Dinwiddie and other governors at Philadelphia to lay plans for the next campaign. Accordingly, Washington asked permission to leave his post and travel northward to see the general. Early in February 1757, Dinwiddie gave Washington leave to go to Philadelphia, but grudgingly. He did not think it necessary for the colonel to confer with Loudoun about military planning; he said nothing concerning the personal fortunes of Washington.

By that time Washington was much less than a friend of Dinwiddie and was behaving as if he were an enemy. Washington's merits had been brought to the attention of Loudoun by several men, among them, perhaps, Dinwiddie, Shirley, William Fairfax, Lord Fairfax, and Thomas Gage, afterward General Gage, who had served with the Virginian in the Braddock campaign. The colonel had not yet abandoned hope for a British commission. On January 28 he wrote to James Cuningham, aide-de-camp of Loudoun, enclosing a letter dated January 15 for the general, together with a memorial from the officers of the Virginia regiment.

Washington probably composed the memorial which again suggested that he and they would be glad to receive appointments from the crown. Offering Loudoun a brief history of the war in Virginia, he described the great hardships encountered by the regiment and emphasized its achievements and competence. He condemned the Virginia assembly because it had not properly supported the troops, because it had only made provision for defense. He said that the French ought to have been attacked.

Those criticisms implied a measure of condemnation of Dinwiddie. But Washington assailed the governor more directly. He revived the suspicion that his own report of French aggression in 1753 had at the time been "thought a fiction, and a scheme to promote the interest of a private company, even by some who had a share in government," a reference that might injure Dinwiddie's reputation. He asserted that "the orders I receive are full of ambiguity. I am left, like a wanderer in the wilderness, to proceed at hazard. I am answerable for consequences, and blamed, without the privilege of defence." He had continued to serve Virginia, he said, only because of the call of duty.

Washington added to this history an ardent appeal to Loudoun in behalf of the Virginia officers. Learning of the appointment of the earl as commander in chief, they "fondly pronounced your Lordship our patron." The name of Loudoun was familiar to him "on account of the important services performed to his Majesty in other parts of the world." Those services were not actually remarkable. "Do not think, my Lord, that I am going to flatter; notwithstanding I have exalted sentiments of your Lordship's character and respect your rank, it is not my intention to adulate. My nature is open and honest and free from guile!"

Commenting on the earlier efforts of the regimental officers to secure British preferment, he declared,

We have, my Lord, ever since our defeat at the Meadows, and, behaviour under his Excellency General Braddock, been tantalized, nay, bid to expect most sanguinely a better establishment,

and have waited in tedious expectation of seeing this accomplished, the assembly, it is true, have, I believe, done every thing
in their power to bring this about; first, by soliciting his Honor,
the Lieutenant-Governor, to address his Majesty; and next by addressing his Majesty themselves in favor of their regiment.

One would not know from this account that Dinwiddie
had been far more active in asserting the merits of the regiment and of Washington than had the burgesses.

"With regard to myself," declared Washington, "I cannot
forbear adding, that, had his Excellency General Braddock
survived his unfortunate defeat, I should have met with
preferment agreeable to my wishes. I had his promise to that
purpose . . . General Shirley was not unkind in his prom-
ises, but he has gone to England."

Washington asserted that he offered a "short and disinterested relation" which "contains no misrepresentations, nor
aggravated relation of facts, nor unjust reflections." Nevertheless, it is apparent, in what he said and in what he did not say,
that he dealt less than fairly with Dinwiddie in a paper submitted to the man who was Dinwiddie's superior as titular
governor of Virginia and whose opinion of Dinwiddie was
still important to the lieutenant governor. Washington had
not yet reached his twenty-fifth birthday. Young, he forgot
the favors he had received from Dinwiddie, remembered more
recent slights, some doubtless fancied rather than intended.

James Cuningham placed the two papers submitted by
Washington in the hands of Lord Loudoun at New York
some time before February 27. He informed Washington
that Loudoun was at the moment too busy to reply, but that
the general seemed "very much pleased with the accounts you
have given him of the situation of our affairs to the south'ard."
No answer in writing has been found. Washington had an in-
terview with Loudoun on March 20, but the general did not
give the Virginia regiment British status, and Washington returned home without a commission from the crown. He knew
before he left Philadelphia that his pleas had been rejected.
Thereafter he was well aware that his hopes of a British appointment had had no substance. One may only speculate
whether the course of Washington's life and the history of

America would have been much different had he indeed become a king's officer.

Dinwiddie was in Philadelphia at the time and in touch
with Loudoun; but so far as the evidence shows he said nothing against Washington to the general. There is, however,
reason to believe that Dinwiddie learned, either directly from
Loudoun or indirectly, about the colonel's letter of January 15. Quite possibly the Scottish commander in chief and
governor of Virginia confided to the Scottish lieutenant governor of Virginia that his behavior had been condemned in
omission and commission by Colonel Washington.

Dinwiddie and Washington continued to bicker in the
campaign of 1757. On June 10, after Washington had to
secure money for his expenses from Dinwiddie, he worried
lest Dinwiddie neglect to supply it promptly. "I am convinced," he wrote John Robinson, "it would give pleasure to
the Governor to hear that I was involved in trouble, however
undeservedly, such are his dispositions toward me." He complained to Dinwiddie late in August that his best efforts did
not please the governor. Washington was then suffering from
the "bloody flux"—dysentery—an ailment that continued to
the end of the campaign, sapped his health, and doubtless affected his spirits. The elderly governor and the sickly colonel
moved toward an open break.

In September Washington received a curious letter from
Captain William Peachey, one of his officers. Peachey reported, at third hand, an allegation by Colonel Richard Corbin to the effect that Washington had manufactured news of
imminent Indian attack in the spring of 1757 in order to
persuade the assembly to give him more men and money, and
that Dinwiddie and other men in Williamsburg, learning of
the deception, had turned against Washington.

Washington concluded that he had indeed been slandered
by Corbin. He undertook, not only to defend himself, but to
ask Dinwiddie why he was no longer in the governor's good
graces. Had Colonel Corbin accused him of such misconduct
to the governor? And why had Dinwiddie turned against him?
"It is evident, from a variety of circumstances, and especially
from the change in your Honor's conduct towards me, that
some person, as well inclined to detract, but better skilled in

the art of detraction, than the author of the above stupid scandal, has made free with my character."

In return Washington received a polite rebuke. Dinwiddie had never heard of the accusation. He knew it to be untrue. "I wou'd advise you not to give notice to every idle story you hear." He also told Washington why he had turned away from the colonel. "My conduct to you from the beginning was always friendly, but you know I had great reason to suspect you of ingratitude, which I am convinc'd your own conscience & reflection must allow. I had reason to be angry, but this endeavor to forget." Dinwiddie was then planning to depart for England. "I wish," he wrote, "my successor may shew you friendship as I have done—I wish you health & happiness."

It is clear enough that Dinwiddie, charging Washington with ingratitude but disposed to let bygones be bygones, referred particularly to Washington's letter to Lord Loudoun of January 15. The colonel, replying, denied that he had returned ill for good. But he also said, "If an open, disinterested behavior carries offence, I may have offended; because I have all along laid it down as a maxim to represent facts freely and impartially, but no more to others, than I have to you, sir." In the same letter Washington petitioned for leave so that he might go from his headquarters at Winchester to Williamsburg to present accounts. The governor refused the request—Washington had no financial business that required his immediate presence in the capital; he had had enough leaves of absence; he was needed on the Virginia frontier.

It may be concluded that the governor then wanted no more to do with Washington than was absolutely necessary. Did he do Washington an injustice by refusing him leave of absence? He did not know that the colonel was ill. Certainly, Washington commented unfairly concerning the refusal, in a letter to John Robinson. He told Robinson he had asked for permission to visit Williamsburg not only to adjust accounts, but "to represent the melancholy situation of our distressed frontiers." But in his request for leave he had said nothing about a need to report on the military situation.

Early in November of 1757 Washington became seriously ill from dysentery. His physician insisted that he abandon his post in order to save his life; he must not remain at Winchester until he could secure permission from Dinwiddie to leave the frontier. Washington reluctantly went without authority to Mount Vernon to recuperate. Learning what had occurred from Captain Robert Stewart, Dinwiddie responded in gentlemanly fashion that "the violent complaint" from which Washington suffered "gives me great concern, it was unknown to me or he shou'd have had leave of absence sooner, & I am very glad he did not delay following the Doctrs. advice, to try a change of air. I sincerely wish him a speedy recovery."

Clearly Dinwiddie, soon to leave Virginia forever, wrote honestly, and clearly he retained respect, even a measure of affection, for Washington, despite their recent disputes. How Washington looked upon Dinwiddie when the Virginian regained health, tranquility, and perspective, no one can say.

Chapter 8
Last Years in Britain

In the company of three other commercial ships bound for Britain, the *Baltimore*, carrying the Dinwiddie family, made its way out from the Virginia capes in the midst of winter. Four days after their departure the four vessels encountered a gale and were separated. However, by February 17, 1758, Captain Cruikshanks brought the *Baltimore* safely into harbor at Portsmouth on the south coast of England, after a fast crossing of five weeks. The Dinwiddies proceeded to London where the governor established his home. He possessed a substantial income, and he lived as comfortably as health and age would permit during twelve years of retirement from public life.

Dinwiddie retained his interest in Virginia and affection for some Virginians. As the Seven Years' War drew to an end and the British government began to reconsider policy regarding the American colonies, he offered peculiarly bad advice to the ministry. For he continued to think as a veteran servant of the crown, disposed to assert the authority of Britain over the colonies, even to increase it. He did not live long enough to read in English newspapers about the clash of arms at Lexington and Concord.

Soon after his arrival in London Dinwiddie made formal calls on various members of the British ministry. "I never was witness to a more kind and favorable reception," reported agent James Abercromby to John Blair. "To thankfull acknowledgments for a wise prudent and rational administration, has been added a very great concern that his health did not permit him to continue longer therein, from such tokens of approbation, and regard, I have reason to conclude that Mr. Dinwiddie's interposition on this or any other occasion will add enough weight to my negotiations." The last was a hint that Virginians would do well to continue to show respect for their former governor. Abercromby similarly assured Colonel Richard Corbin that Dinwiddie could exert influence at Whitehall. However, Dinwiddie did not immediately get to see William Pitt, the great minister who had assumed direction of the British war effort. Pitt was suffering from the gout.

Dinwiddie himself was in poor condition, so he said in a letter to his friend, the Reverend Thomas Dawson. He consulted a physician who advised him to go to Bath for treatment and recuperation. But the strains of a midwinter voyage across the Atlantic apparently did not affect him much. Release from his duties in Virginia was beneficial. Abercromby reported that the governor was "rather better than worse, since his arrival in England, being at rest, he may get the better of his complaint in some degree, tho' it is partly the effect of old age."

The opinion and prognosis offered by Abercromby were undoubtedly correct. On March 27, 1758 the Bath *Journal*, which routinely announced the arrival of important visitors, reported the coming of "Governor Dinwiddie, lady, and daughter." Conceivably, he met there Francis Fauquier, who had been chosen as his successor and whose appearance at Bath had been mentioned in the same newspaper on February 20.

Presumably the governor profited from his stay at Bath, for he was well enough to undertake one journey to Scotland, an arduous enterprise at that time. His native country received him with pleasure. He was given the freedom of the burgh of Dumfries, home of his Dinwiddie ancestors. Both he and his brother Lawrence were granted honorary citizenship in Edinburgh. Even the governor's daughter, Rebecca, was chivalrously tendered the privileges of a burgess of Renfrew. To a degree the governor could return favors extended to him and his—he lent the city of Glasgow £1,000 in the following year.

Before he returned to London in the autumn of 1758 Dinwiddie traveled 1,300 miles, a performance which suggests that his physical troubles were vexing rather than truly alarming. But they did not vanish. From London in November he wrote in a tremulous, uncertain script to Colonel Corbin, "My health continues but very poorly." In February 1760 he said in a letter to Governor Horatio Sharpe, "I have been in poor health ever since my arrival, have been twice at Bath, & am advised to try the waters once more." He continued to visit Bath frequently, at least once in each year (except 1762) from 1758 to 1765.

Early in February 1768 it was reported from London, "We hear that Robert Dinwiddie, Esq., late Governour of Virginia, who lay dangerously ill, and attended by several physicians, at his house in Pall Mall, is now in a fair way of recovery." By June he was well enough to travel with his family to Clifton, near Bristol to seek surcease at the Hot Wells of that resort. He and his family went to Clifton again in the early summer of 1769.

The Dinwiddies maintained social and business contacts with Virginia relatives and friends. They entertained sons of John Blair and Colonel Corbin who came to England for advanced schooling. The governor corresponded with Blair and Corbin; his wife wrote to Virginia ladies about her and their domestic concerns. Dinwiddie arranged to send presents of a cheese, some porter, and a chest of lemons to Corbin. The colonel sold the slaves and household goods that Dinwiddie had left behind in Williamsburg.

Corbin also collected many thousands of pounds from Virginians who were indebted to the governor, a task that occupied some of Corbin's time and energy for a full decade. With characteristic generosity Dinwiddie authorized Corbin to reduce an obligation of Mr. Tayloe, "as I have a very great value and esteem for him," and to be gentle in dealing with other Virginians in his debt. Dinwiddie recommended Corbin for an appointment as receiver general of the quitrents in Virginia, and Corbin secured it. As "a near relation" of Dinwiddie, Corbin received a present of a silver tea table.

Corbin sought more substantial benefit from his connection with the former governor. Dinwiddie still owned the surveyor generalship of the customs in the southern district. In July 1765 Corbin reported that Peter Randolph was gravely ill. Corbin hastened to send the news, "as this is an event that will affect your family." Corbin asked Dinwiddie to "think of my son to succeed on such conditions of advantage to your family as you think reasonable." Corbin's son did not get Randolph's job.

In June 1768 Corbin asked Dinwiddie for larger reward for his many services. Since Dinwiddie was never niggardly, it is altogether likely that Corbin was paid for his trouble. Another Virginian who sought the help of Dinwiddie toward securing a British appointment was Edward Hack Mosely. He desired to be either naval officer or collector of customs at Norfolk in 1769, and asked Dinwiddie to exert influence in his behalf.

That Dinwiddie actually did help Virginia friends to obtain British appointments, records do not say. He recommended Governor Horatio Sharpe for a lieutenant colonelcy in the British army, without success. A committee of the Ohio Company urged Dinwiddie, in 1761, to do what he could to secure a deed from the crown that would strengthen the claim of the company to lands in the Ohio Valley. The documents do not testify that he was active in its behalf; they do relate that he went to government offices in London in the early months of his retirement to give advice concerning Virginia.

If Dinwiddie was graciously received in London after his final return from Virginia, nevertheless he apparently did not enjoy the highest favor among all the king's advisers. The fact that he was not permitted to call on William Pitt may be significant. Pitt may well have been aware of the denunciations of Dinwiddie sent to London by Lord Loudoun. Certainly the government ignored a petition presented by the former governor in 1759 asking a reward for his services. Dinwiddie sought an annuity of £400 per annum. Governor Gooch had been given such a grant. Dinwiddie contended that an inquiry "into a life spent in the public service" would justify the annuity. Had his health permitted him to remain in Virginia, "this application would never have been made." He renewed his request in 1761, again without success. It may be that his life tenancy of the surveyor generalship for the southern colonies was thought to be a sufficient reward for a man who had done his duty but had not been spectacularly successful in Williamsburg.

Certainly Dinwiddie turned against Pitt. Just as certainly he continued to be an ardent advocate for exercise of British authority over the American colonies at the close of the Seven Years' War. He may have had somewhat to do with the making of a new British policy that ultimately led to American rebellion and independence: He was one of those who advised the British ministry to impose the hated stamp taxes.

As the end of the war approached, in January 1763 Dinwiddie offered advice to the earl of Bute, prime minister and favorite of George III, about policy regarding America. He endorsed a ministerial decision to keep Canada rather than return it to France in exchange for a tropical island or islands in the Caribbean Sea. Bourbon possessions in that sea could easily be conquered in the future, were it highly desirable to seize them, but the French in Canada had been formidable. Should they be permitted to retain Canada, they would be so again.

Britain, according to Dinwiddie, had been lucky in the Seven Years' War in North America: New York had been saved from the French by accident; Nova Scotia had been preserved by an impetuous naval officer; the outcome was a mere "issue of chance"; Britain's triumphs were accidental, "tho' they have been taken up as the fruitful topicks of panegyrics upon a certain great man." So much for Pitt, the great war minister.

For the future, Dinwiddie urged that both the proprietary and corporate colonies be royalized, and that all the governors in the Thirteen Colonies meet every three years to consider their common problems. Trade with the Indians should be put in the hands of public officials, since it was a matter of "national" concern—Dinwiddie placed peace on the frontier above the benefits of private enterprise.

The retired governor also resurrected and elaborated his scheme of 1756 for establishing a new colony somewhere beyond the Appalachians. It would serve, of course, as a buffer against Indian attacks. The colony should be located in "a township upon the Ohio, or one of the lakes." It should be peopled in part by soldiers released from service in Europe at the end of the war. They would be more comfortable and useful in the American wilderness "than in a brothel in Drury

Lane, or a Magdalene house" in London. Wives could be found for them. "The Indian women have their ears sufficiently open to the solicitations of white men, and no wonder" in view of "the coldness of their copper coloured gallants." Besides, said Dinwiddie, there were ill-favored white women in the colonies who would also be glad to marry soldiers. It would cost £30,000 per annum during a period of three years to establish the colony.

Whence should come that money? Dinwiddie suggested that Parliament should require the Americans to pay "a stamp duty on all bonds obligations and other instruments of writing," stamp taxes similar to those collected in Britain. Such a levy would bring forth the needed cash.

It would be quite unreasonable to infer that Robert Dinwiddie, putting forward his notions regarding British policy toward America, was principally responsible for the measures undertaken by Britain immediately after the Seven Years' War. Most of his proposals were not adopted. Others were not exclusively his brainchildren. A stamp tax had long been urged as a means of extracting revenue from the colonists, and thought of one was in the very air of London. Dinwiddie may have given a little push to men contemplating levies upon the Americans.

In any event, the former governor, in British tranquility, clearly continued to believe that British authority must be exerted over the Thirteen Colonies as never before. It seems not to have occurred to him that British subjects living beyond the Atlantic ought to be considered as the equals of subjects who happened to reside in the mother country, much less that they must be so treated if the empire was to endure on the western side of the ocean.

What he thought about American resistance against the exercise of British power in the crises that developed in 1765 and in 1768, documents do not tell us. But he most likely favored repression of the rebellious colonists. He was doubtless too old, too much in the habit of asserting and defending British authority, to change his outlook. An old-school imperialist, his allegiance had always belonged to the crown and to Parliament.

Little more remains to record concerning Robert Dinwiddie. It would appear that he reduced his business activities as the end of his life approached. A firm known as Dinwiddie, Crawford & Company was busily engaged in trade between Glasgow and Virginia between the close of the Seven Years' War and the outbreak of the War of Independence. Its principal founder, however, was not Robert, but Robert's brother, Lawrence, whose death occurred in 1764. Before Lawrence died, Robert sold his share in their delftware pottery in Glasgow. He remained prosperous.

On July 16, 1770, the Bath *Journal* again announced that Governor Dinwiddie had arrived at the Hot Wells of Clifton. He died at that place in his lodgings on July 27, at the age of 77, and was buried with some pomp in the parish church of Clifton. His widow and his daughters erected a memorial in stone to his memory.

In this church are deposited the remains of Robert Dinwiddie, Esq'r formerly Governor of Virginia, who deceased July 27, 1770, in the 78th year of his age. The annals of that country will testify with what judgment, activity and zeal he exerted himself in the publick cause, when the whole North American continent was involved in a French and Indian War. His rectitude of conduct in his government, and integrity in other publick employments, add a lustre to his character, which was revered while he lived, and will be held in estimation while his name survives. His more private virtues, and the amiable social qualities he possess'd, were the happiness of his numerous friends and relations, many of whom shared his bounty; all lament his loss. As his happy disposition for domestic life were best known to his affectionate wife and daughters, they have erected this monument to the memory of his conjugal and paternal love, which they will ever cherish and revere with that piety and tenderness he so greatly merited.

Farewell, blest shade! no more with grief opprest,
Propitious angels guide thee to thy rest!

It is not expected that an epitath should tell the whole truth about a departed mortal. In their grief, survivors of a dead man remember his virtues. But other evidence survives that Dinwiddie was highly respected in Britain. The London *Chronicle*, reporting his death, gave him a paragraph of praise. He was distinguished for "uprightness, integrity, and abilities." He "gained universal respect and esteem in private and public life." He was "ever ready to give assistance to the distressed, so he always gave it with a sincerity and chearfulness that became an honest good heart; in short, he was a good man, and a good Christian."

Dinwiddie left a handsome estate. In his probated will, dated May 2, 1769, the governor, then residing in Saint Albans Street in the city of Westminster, made bequests to various relatives and friends; gave £100 to the University of Glasgow for the purchase of books; and donated £50 for the relief of distressed citizens of his native city. To each of his daughters he bequeathed £10,000. To his widow he gave an annuity of £350 per annum, all his household goods, and the income from £1,000 held in trust and from his house and lot in Bermuda during her lifetime. She survived him by many years, dying in London in February 1793.

There are now no direct descendants of Robert Dinwiddie. His older daughter Elizabeth died a spinster at the age of 35 in 1773 and was buried at Clifton near her father. Rebecca Dinwiddie married Archibald Hamilton of the Isle of Man at the fashionable St. Margaret's Church in London in August, 1771. But she had no children. The memory of Robert Dinwiddie is proudly preserved among the numerous progeny of his siblings. No one can say that he does not deserve to be so remembered.

A Note on the Sources

It is possible in this note to mention only the principal sources for the life of Robert Dinwiddie. Scholars who wish to verify information or to reconsider interpretations offered in the biography may consult the author's typescript copy, with specific citations, preserved in the archives of Colonial Williamsburg.

This brief biography is based largely on official records. Only a part of Dinwiddie's private correspondence, which must have been very extensive, is available. In consequence, neither his early life nor his last years can be described in detail; indeed, one could wish for more information concerning his career as a servant of the crown. It is to be hoped that additional manuscripts will appear in the future to throw still brighter light upon him and his important career.

Although this book is primarily founded on contemporary records, the author has, of course, profited from the labors of other scholars, especially from Louis K. Koontz, *Robert Dinwiddie* . . . (Glendale, California, 1941). The present study contains some information not to be found in the biography by Professor Koontz and corrects some errors in it. Even so, Professor Koontz's pioneering work smoothed the way for the author of this volume and, perhaps, for a still better life of Dinwiddie to come.

The author also derived substantial help from Henry C. Wilkinson's history of early Bermuda; Richard Morton's history of Virginia; the biography of Lord Loudoun by Stanley M. Pargellis; the multi-volume history of the British empire during the third quarter of the eighteenth century by Lawrence H. Gipson; the study of royal government in the southern colonies in *The Quest for Power* by Jack P. Greene; the scholarly examination by George M. Brydon of the Anglican church in Virginia; accounts of the pistole fee controversy by Glenn C. Smith and Jack P. Greene; and the valuable analysis of the "Dinwiddieana" in the Henry E. Huntington Library and Art Gallery by Richard Beale Davis.

A search in Glasgow and Edinburgh for manuscripts concerning the early life of Dinwiddie brought scanty results. However, valuable materials concerning his family, birthdate, and schooling were found in the Lockhart Family Papers, preserved by Colonial Williamsburg; James R. Anderson and James Gourlay, *The Provosts of Glasgow from 1609 to 1832* (Glasgow, n.d.); Cosmo Innes (ed.), *Munimenta Universitatis Glasguensis . . . 3* (Glasgow, 1854); W. Innes Addison (comp.), *A Roll of the Graduates of the University of Glasgow From 31st December, 1727 to 31st December, 1897* (Glasgow, 1898); and *Notes and Queries*, Sixth Series, 8 (1883): 113.

There are many references to Dinwiddie as a resident of Bermuda in the correspondence of the governors of that colony preserved in Colonial Office, 37: 1–26, and 38: 8, 10, 12, British Public Record Office. Examination of these confirmed the findings of Henry C. Wilkinson concerning the Bermudian career of Dinwiddie and brought forth a few additional details.

The appointments and activities of Dinwiddie as surveyor general and inspector general are recorded in the contemporary official documents printed in the *Acts of the Privy Council, Colonial Series; Calendar of State Papers, America & West Indies; Journals of the Commissioners of Trade and Plantations;* and *Calendar of Treasury Books and Papers.* His reports on the customs service, trade, and imperial problems are to be found in Colonial Office, 5: 5 and 152; 28: 25; Treasury, 1; and the William L. Clements Library.

Only a few issues have survived of the *Virginia Gazette* printed during the sojourns of Dinwiddie in the Old Dominion. They contain some useful references to the governor. Many items concerning him are scattered through the *Virginia Magazine of History and Biography* and also in the *William and Mary Quarterly.* Other important published references to Governor Dinwiddie are to be found in Jack P. Greene (ed.), *The Diary of Landon Carter;* George W. Pilcher (ed.), *The Reverend Samuel Davies Abroad: The Diary of a Journey to England and Scotland, 1753-55;* Richard Beale Davis (ed.), "The Colonial Virginia Satirist: Mid-Eighteenth Century Commentary on Politics, Religion, and Society," *Transactions of the American Philosophical Society,* New Series, 57, Part 1 (1967): 5-74; and Stanley M. Pargellis (ed.), *Military Affairs in North America, 1748-1765.* For relations between Dinwiddie and George Washington, John C. Fitzpatrick (ed.), *The Writings of George Washington* and Stanislaus M. Hamilton (ed.), *Letters to Washington and Accompanying Papers,* are indispensable.

The official records of Governor Dinwiddie, the Council, and the House of Burgesses are, of course, of the first importance. The *Executive Journals of the Council of Colonial Virginia* and the *Journals of the House of Burgesses* are available in print, and laws enacted during Dinwiddie's time may be consulted in Hening's *Statutes.* A substantial body of Dinwiddie items is housed in the Henry E. Huntington Library and Art Gallery.

Above all other sources in value for study of Dinwiddie's governorship are his letters and papers. The basic correspondence of Dinwiddie with the British secretaries of state and the Board of Trade and other papers concerning Dinwiddie are preserved in the Public Record Office in Colonial Office 5: 6, 17, 1325–1338, 1344; 324: 38; and Treasury 1: 348, 358, 360, 372, 1324, 3818. The reports of Dinwiddie to the bishop of London are preserved in the Fulham Papers, Lambeth Palace. Many of the manuscripts listed are also available in the form of transcripts and microfilms in the Library of Congress and especially in Virginia repositories. The Dinwiddie letterbooks housed in the Virginia Historical Society contain drafts of most of the official letters sent by the governor to London and also of many other public and private letters to officials and other persons both in London and America during the period 1754–58. These papers, with a few additions and helpful introductory material, have been edited by R. A. Brock and published by the Virginia Historical Society in two volumes as *The Official Papers of Robert Dinwiddie.*

Materials concerning Dinwiddie's last years in Britain are scanty. The James Abercromby Letterbook, preserved in the Virginia State Library, and in microfilm at Colonial Williamsburg, contains some information. The Colonel Richard Corbin Letterbook at Colonial Williamsburg, containing copies of letters from Corbin to Dinwiddie, is very useful. The petition of Dinwiddie to Lord Bute of June 22, 1761, is in the British Museum, Additional Manuscripts, 5, 726, folio 92. The paper submitted by Dinwiddie to Lord Bute concerning American policy of January 17, 1763, is in the British Museum, Additional Manuscripts, 38, 334, folios 297–300. A microfilm copy of it is available at Colonial Williamsburg. A few references to Dinwiddie appear in *The London Magazine*, *The Gentleman's Magazine*, *The London Chronicle*, *The Bath Journal*, and *Felix Farley's Bristol Journal*. His illness of 1768 is mentioned in *The Virginia Gazette* (Purdie and Dixon), April 28, 1768. The death of Mrs. Dinwiddie is reported in the *Scots Magazine*, 55 (1793): 102.

Index

Ohio Company, 42, 45, 49–51, 113
Ohio Valley, 39, 40, 42–45, 48, 50, 114
Orme, Captain Robert, 53
Oswego, N.Y., 69
Othello, 18
Ottawa Indians, 40

Parkman, Francis, 90
Parson's Cause, 25
Peachey, Captain William, 107
Pelham, Henry, 12, 14
Penn family, 65, 81, 83–84
Philadelphia, Pa., 70, 79, 80, 104, 106, 107
Pistole fee dispute, 20–21, 24–25, 26–36
Pitt, William, 71, 73, 83, 85, 113, 114
Popple, Governor Alured, 8, 9
Portsmouth, England, 12
Presqu'Isle, Pa., 40, 41, 44

Quakers, 41, 65, 82
Quebec (city), 40
Quebec (province), 38, 39, 50

Ramsay, William, 104
Randolph, Edmund, 5
Randolph family, 17, 23, 28
Randolph, Peter, 13, 63, 112
Randolph, Peyton, 28, 30–33, 35, 47, 78
Rawlings, William, 12–13
Redstone Creek, 45
Rider, Sir Dudley, 28
Robinson, Beverley, 101
Robinson, John, 1, 20, 25, 35, 92; power of, 28, 30, 36–37; condemns Dinwiddie, 78; befriends Washington, 100–108
Robinson, Sir Thomas, 85, 86, 98
St. Clair, John, 51, 68
Saint Kitts, island of, 12
Saint Lawrence River, 38, 86
Saint Pierre, M. de, 44
Saponey Indians, 73
Sharpe, Lieutenant Governor Horatio, 34, 48, 50, 60, 64, 74, 99, 112, 113
Shawnee Indians, 39, 60, 62, 69, 70
Shenandoah Valley, 38, 72, 102
Sherlock, Bishop Thomas, 24, 27
Shirley, General William, 53, 59, 63, 64, 76, 96, 98–99

Shirley, William, Jr., 55
Six Nations, 42–43
Sparks, Jared, 90
Stamp duties, 114, 115
Stanwix, General John, 72
Stephen, Colonel Adam, 61, 98, 99
Stewart, Captain Robert, 109
Stith, Reverend William, 23–24, 27, 28
Stuart, Dr. John, 4
Stuart, Reverend Andrew, 4

Tayloe, Mr., 112
Thomson, James, 9
Tucker family, 8, 10, 28
Tucker, John, 8
Tuscarora Indians, 72

Upton, Arthur, 12–13

Villiers, Louis Coulon de, 46
"Virginia-Centinel No. X," 103
Virginia *Gazette*, 102–103

Wabash River, 39
Walpole, Horatio, 7, 9, 14, 16
Walpole, Sir Robert, 7
Washington, Augustine, 103
Washington, George, 2, 14, 78; and beginning of Seven Years' War, 44–47, 50; in Braddock campaign, 54, 57, 58, 61; defends Virginia frontier, 61–62, 66, 69, 70, 73; relationship with Dinwiddie, 90-109
Washington, Lawrence, 90–91
Wetherburn's Tavern, Williamsburg, 1
Whitefield, Reverend George, 21, 22
Wilkes, John, 2
William and Mary, College of, 18, 21, 23, 24, 27, 38, 68, 91
Williamsburg, 1, 10, 11, 15, 19, 20, 26, 27, 65, 68, 69, 71, 73, 90, 99, 100, 102, 104, 108, 113; Indians at, 62; panic at, 66; Dinwiddie leaves, 75
Wills Creek, 45, 47
Winchester, Va., 58, 61, 62, 70, 73, 108, 109
Wythe, George, 30

Yorktown, Va., 1
Young, Colonel John, 71